GOODYEAR SERIES IN AMERICAN SOCIETY
Jonathan H. Turner, Editor

INEQUALITY: PRIVILEGE & POVERTY IN AMERICA
Jonathan H. Turner and Charles E. Starnes

Forthcoming volumes will include perspectives on:

Women in America
Crime in America
Social Stratification in America
Urban Problems in America

INEQUALITY:
PRIVILEGE & POVERTY
IN AMERICA

INEQUALITY:
PRIVILEGE & POVERTY
IN AMERICA

Jonathan H. Turner & Charles E. Starnes
University of California

Goodyear Publishing Company, Inc.,   Pacific Palisades, California

Library of Congress Cataloging in Publication Data

Turner, Jonathan H
     Inequality: privilege & poverty in America.

     (Goodyear series in American society)
     Includes index.
     1. Wealth—United States.   2. Income distribution—
United States.   3. Poor—United States.   4. Public
welfare—United States.   I. Starnes, Charles E., joint
author.   II. Title.
HC110.W4T86   330.1'6   75-20583
ISBN 0-87620-418-3

330.16
T948i

Library of Congress Catalog Card Number:
75-20583

ISBN: 0-87620-418-3
Y-4183-3

Current Printing (last digit):
10 9 8 7 6 5 4 3 2 1

Printed in the United States of America

76-5474

CONTENTS

INEQUALITY:
PRIVILEGE & POVERTY
IN AMERICA

1
ANALYZING INEQUALITY

ELEMENTARY PRINCIPLES OF INEQUALITY

> *From each according to his*
> *ability, to each according*
> *to his needs*
>
> Marx

In only the simplest societies has this famous Marxian dictum held true. If present-day hunting and gathering societies offer a clue to the past, we can reasonably speculate that human evolution has been guided by Marx's formula for the good society. Until only a few thousand years ago—ten to fifteen thousand at most—human societies were able to extract human effort on the basis of ability and distribute resources on the basis of need. There simply was not enough surplus to hoard, and each person was vitally needed to perpetuate the survival of the small bands of proto-hominids that constituted the first human societies.

Although we can only speculate about early human groups, these first societies were probably cooperative, democratic, and egalitarian. People's natural ability to help the group survive determined their prestige and perhaps their authority. But it is likely that such prestige and authority did not entitle the individual to a larger than average share of the group's scarce resources; all probably shared in these as their needs required. It is easy to romanticize "the noble savage," as many otherwise sophisticated scholars once did, but most early human societies were often engaged in a desperate struggle for survival. People may have shared the society's resources equally, but they did so out of self-interest rather than altruism. Cooperating and sharing in the band were necessary if one was to survive the vicissitudes of the natural environment.[1]

In the struggle to survive in an often hostile environment, instincts for self-preservation probably carried a selective advantage for both individuals and the group. Those individual organisms that did not have a desire to live, to overcome obstacles, and to cope with the hostile environment (many of the first proto-hominids venturing out on the savannah probably did not) got eaten up, thus killing themselves and making a social grouping less viable. But those aggressive, less fearful, more assertive individuals had a selective advantage on the savannah, and hence, they and the groups in which they were implicated survived. Ten million years of such selection of tenacious organisms, willing and capable of living in groups and cooperating, certainly programmed humans—that is, selected for preservation certain genetic codes—into their present profile, despite the fact that many of the conditions that caused this selection have now, of course, vanished. It seems unlikely that humans could have survived and evolved without tenacity and willingness to use their intellectual and physical resources. Those early beings whose desire for survival led them to form cooperative groups were able to survive; others were not. Cooperative, communal, and democratic societies were survival techniques and were not necessarily products of goodness or gregariousness.

When increases in the economic surplus were generated by the application of human intellect and effort to problems of survival, self-interest quite naturally led individuals to seek some of this new surplus. The production of more than was absolutely necessary for survival created a basic problem: Who should get how much? Under conditions of surplus and individual self-interest, competition for shares of the surplus surely began to increase. Previously humans had struggled collectively for survival. Certainly this effort did not diminish, but a new struggle for greater shares of the surplus emerged in human societies. This competition inevitably established winners and losers. Even the simplest human groups exhibit competition for prestige and authority. But as a result of the existence of surplus, a form of inequality based on the distribution of economic goods began to typify human societies. This inequality made terms like *poverty* and *privilege* meaningful, as some came to hoard more economic goods and resources than others.

Economic inequality begets other forms of inequality that, in turn, are likely to increase economic inequality. Those who have the most goods and resources are often able to buy power. That is, they can spend their resources in ways that enable them to induce and force others to comply with their wishes. Properly used, power can generate more surplus, which can buy even more power in a cycle of increasing inequality.

One of the many keys to maintaining power and privilege, as Gerhard Lenski so aptly stated,[2] is the creation and dissemination of ideas that justify and legitimate inequality. If economic inequality can be made to seem right and proper, the need for coercion and the high costs of the use of coercion are diminished. In the evolution of human societies, the unequal distribution of valued economic resources has been accompanied increasingly by the dissemination of ideas that seem to legitimate the control of wealth by few. Once inequality is legitimated by ideas, the power of the wealthy is dramatically increased. They no longer must expend as many of their resources on forcing acceptance of their privilege; they can now use their increased power to gather even more of the economic surplus.

In this scenario of the development of inequality in human affairs can be found several principles on which we can base an analysis of inequality in highly complex societies like the United States:[3] (1) Economic surplus creates distribution problems. (2) Self-interest as conditioned by thousands of years of struggle for survival leads people to a new struggle: the competition for the surplus. (3) Those who win in this competition are able to buy power that can be used to maintain or increase their advantage. (4) To decrease their reliance on force, and to increase the amount of power that can be devoted to securing wealth, the privileged usually seek, through the use of ideas, to mitigate the inherent conflict of interest between themselves and those who are less privileged. Open revolt has often disrupted this process, but the new winners of this competition have typically sought to consolidate power and economic privilege for themselves.

Understanding inequality requires more conceptual elaboration, however, because the dynamics of inequality in complex societies are guided only in the most general way by these principles. Indeed, these elementary principles do not tell us much about the specifics of their application for a particular society at a given time in its history. Instead, they indicate what to look for when studying the unequal distribution of valuable resources.

To refine these principles, we must apply them to the analysis of a large number of concrete societies. As the complexity of the distribution systems in societies becomes evident, a more detailed model of inequality for a given society can be constructed. If equivalent societies can be subjected to similar analysis, then a sophisticated theory of inequality can be developed. This book seeks to begin such a process by analyzing inequality in the United States. Specifically we will ask: How much inequality is there? How long has the present profile of inequality existed? How do our elementary principles help us understand this profile and its tenure? Can we develop a model of inequality in America that can contribute to the development of a more general theory of inequality?

PROBLEMS IN STUDYING INEQUALITY

Inequality and Stratification

The analysis of inequality requires at least one elementary conceptual distinction between *inequality* and *stratification*. In our analysis, *inequality* will refer to the *pattern of distribution* of economic goods in a society. We use inequality to denote the unequal distribution of wealth and other economic assets to different positions in the society. In a study of stratification, questions about the emergence of unequal positions, the respective degrees of prestige accorded them, the life styles of occupants of these positions, and the mobility of people to and from positions would dominate the analysis. In this study, we are concerned only with the fact that a system of positions receiving different proportions of economic surplus persists in a particular pattern. We will not discuss such processes as socialization and discrimination, nor will we discuss how such processes affect an individual's mobility from one position to another, as would be done in a stratification analysis.[4]

In the chapters to follow, we seek to understand how wealth—money or any good that can be converted to money—is unequally distributed to different positions in American society. For convenience and efficiency, we often group similar positions into analytical categories—such as "social class," "the poor," "the affluent," "the rich," and so forth. We do not focus on the cultures, experiences, life styles, and other sociocultural characteristics that typify various groups and categories of positions in American society. Our guiding question is much more limited: What processes maintain the relative degrees of wealth received by different segments of the population in American society?[5]

The reason for this limited approach is simple: We believe that it is necessary to understand the profile of inequality in America *before* an adequate analysis of stratification questions can be undertaken. A cynic once remarked that money isn't everything, but what it isn't it can buy. Who has how much of the wealth and income in American society determines, in large part, the distribution of power, prestige, health, education, and other resources. Thus, the examination of stratification questions can be more meaningful after the forces that affect the distribution of economic assets to various segments of the society are comprehended.

Problems of Bias

Economic inequality reflects differences in political power among a population. This should alert us to the problems of gathering, reporting, and analyzing data on economic inequality. Since it is the government that gathers the data on inequality, would not its gathering and reporting reflect, to some extent, the biases of those with the most political power and privilege? Would there not be a vested interest in suppressing data that would expose the true amount of inequality in a society? Only a partial "yes" can be given to these questions, because the government has collected *some* data on the distribution of wealth and income in America. But there is surprisingly little government information on wealth distribution, and none that is recent. It is, of course, impossible to know if and how suppression has occurred, but it is clear that there is an interesting lack of evidence on wealth distribution. Fortunately, as we show in Chapter 3, there is considerably more information about the yearly incomes of people in America. But even here, some noticeable omissions are evident.

We have argued that inequality is legitimated by ideas. This approach indicates the ideological implications of our analysis. Despite our intentions to suspend bias with respect to questions of inequality, we are inexorably drawn into political processes and ideological issues. Thus, before beginning our detailed analysis of the distribution of wealth and income in America, we examine some of the political and ideological implications of this analysis.

In every society, those who belong to the dominant social classes have the greatest capacity to create and disseminate social theories that explain and rationalize the prevailing system of inequality. At all times and places in recorded history, we find accounts of the origins, the nature, and the appropriateness of existing systems of social inequality. And yet, despite the perils of too vocal dissent in some societies, we also find these accounts of inequality challenged. Gerhard Lenski[6] has noted a general historical dialectic between supportive and challenging accounts of social inequality. Each of these orientations has had several variant formulations, and each has had its periods of waxing and waning. But neither remains dormant for long, because there is always a dialectical tendency for periods of domination by one account to call forth a revival of the other.

Lenski has suggested that the supportive orientation presents the "conservative thesis" and that the challenging orientation presents the "radical antithesis." The most obvious contrast between the two has been the apparent egalitarianism of the radical antithesis as opposed to the status quo defenses of the conservative thesis. But in actual fact, it is typically an illusion that elitism is any less a part of the radical challenge than of the conservative defense. Radicals ordinarily attack a specific brand of institutionalized inequality rather than the principle of inequality.

The conservative and radical theses differ on several basic issues concerning the nature of humanity, the nature of society, and their interrelation. Conservative theory has tended to see social institutions as the source of the nobler sentiments and actions of humanity and, correspondingly, has stressed the darker aspects of human nature and the role of social institutions in restraining their expression. In contrast, radicals have taken an ambivalent stance on these matters. They tend to view human nature in more optimistic terms and to envision possibilities for a new and good society. But they see social institutions as instruments by which the ruling class oppresses human nature and its fuller realization. Because elites use institutions to oppress, radicals view the social institutions of the existing social order as rooted in the baser greeds of humanity.

Conservatives see great merit in existing social institutions and value persons who hold positions of power and leadership within those institutions. And so conservatives propose that the forms of inequality expressed in social institutions are natural, just, and inevitable. They discount the use of force and coercion in social affairs and stress the effects of differences in virtue, talent, ability, and merit in determining careers and fortunes (or misfortunes).

Radicals reverse these judgments. They do not ordinarily reject the argument that positions of power and leadership *should* be awarded on the basis of merit. Rather, they assert that, in the current system, merit is not the basis of power and leadership. Radicals reject the notion that there is a correspondence between the pattern of inequality—that is, who gets how much—and the abilities and contributions to society of people at various levels of income and wealth. They believe that social institutions express current inequalities and are unnatural perpetuators of injustices. Radicals see inequality and present social institutions as mutually reenforcing, and so they propose a reconstruction of social institutions to reduce the amount of inequality. These proposals usually give special emphasis to the intrinsic conflict in social affairs and, particularly, to the significance of coercion and exploitation as the sources of power and privilege in a society.

The roots of the conservative and radical theses on social inequality go at least as far back as ancient Greece. Aristotle might well be called the original ideologist of the middle class in Western thought, although his conservative theory supported the richest class as well. He held that all societies are divided into the rich, the poor, and the mean, or middle, classes. The middle class was, for Aristotle, characterized by rational and moderate tendencies and was thus the proper foundation for the good society. In many respects, his views were based on the general features of his own society. An empirical and practical thinker, he was inclined to believe in the status quo. This propensity led him to support the rich as well as the middle class and even to support their rationalizations of slavery and private property.

Plato's radical antithesis—radical, that is, in the context of the time—contrasted with Aristotle's conservative thesis. Plato, too, thought in terms of a three-class system, although he divided the upper class of guardians into ruling and nonruling groups. Each class in Plato's system was assigned its proper function. Ruling guardians were to be denied property beyond the bare essentials so that they would not be corrupted by rule. Equal opportunity to become guardians was to be assured by common socialization of all children, and elevation to guardianship was to be granted only on the basis of merit. Plato's theory of classes was designed both as a critique and a utopian proposal. But it was only contextually egalitarian, because it said little about the poor and, in fact, excluded some people entirely.

Classification of a particular version of social inequality as within the radical or conservative tradition is sometimes arbitrary. In part, this is because social structures, and hence social thought, are continually subject to change. What appears radical at one point in time may appear conservative at another. Indeed, the use of the term *radical* may be misleading. Many of the arguments so labeled might more appropriately be called *reformist*, to emphasize that they call less for abolition of inequality than for the abolition of inequity. A cursory glance at the history of revolutions reveals that it has been less a history of abolition than of reallocation. The English, French, Russian, and Chinese revolutions did not result in the abolition of inequality, although each represents a radical attack on a structure of power and privilege. Nor, for all of de Tocqueville's celebrations of American egalitarianism,[7] was the American revolution different. We agree with Lenski that the social dialectic of historical conflicts has tended to push theories into either the conservative or radical attitude, but we do not feel that these labels are useful in organizing a brief account of the major developments in theories of inequality. The radical and conservative labels are best reserved for distinguishing the major contending theories in the dynamics of specific societies or eras.[8]

Nevertheless, within the context of contemporary views on the system of inequality in the United States, we prefer to take up the radical thesis. As we argued earlier, all societies with economic surplus possess systems of inequality. Each system produces a dominant class with a dominant ideology that justifies the structure and consequences of the system. The dominant ideology of this class in the United States is, as we will see, an ideology of inequality, even though it is cloaked in a rhetoric of equality and equity. Americans have long been infatuated with the belief that America is an egalitarian society unlike any since prehistory. Especially important is the claim that equality of opportunity exists for all who seek it and that failure to rise to the top of the social pyramid results from lack of ambition, talent, or perseverance. Such claims are, as we analyze in detail in later chapters, reflections of the dominant values in America.

Such ideological presuppositions not only blame the victims of inequality for their fate but praise the benefactors for their privilege. As if to codify the matter, Americans appear to glorify and emulate the leisure class.[9] The heads of domestic political and economic empires are enshrined in placenames, monuments, and popular biographies. Writers who remind us of our longstanding "American dilemma,"[10] and domestic journalists who on occasion rediscover the "other America"[11] of poverty, are scarcely read and rarely recognized. In the end, Americans declare themselves to be the first new nation and applaud the miracles of economic progress and political democracy afforded by an escape from history's legacy of inequality.

It is in this ideological and political context, then, that this book on inequality in America must be evaluated. Those who analyze the amount of inequality and the ways that dominant values and beliefs legitimate economic and political arrangements that maintain inequality are, by definition, radicals. Such probing and exploring can easily be described as an attempt to challenge. In examining the system of economic distribution and questioning why the data are so incomplete, we become critics. Thus, even though we seek to remain objective and to report the facts as we see them, our analysis of the evidence on inequality will lead some to place us in the radical camp. The fact that we go willingly into this camp reveals a source of potential bias that must be critically assessed by the reader. It is with these warnings, then, that we now undertake a detailed look at the evidence on inequality in America.

NOTES

1. For a more detailed comparative analysis, see: Jonathan H. Turner, *Patterns of Social Organization* (New York: McGraw-Hill, 1972); Gerhard Lenski, *Power and Privilege* (New York: McGraw-Hill, 1966); Manning Nash, *Primitive and Peasant Economic Systems* (San Francisco: Chandler, 1966); M. G. Bicchieri, ed., *Hunters and Gatherers Today* (New York: Holt, Rinehart, and Winston, 1972); and Richard B. Lee and Irven DeVore, eds., *Man the Hunter* (Chicago: Aldine, 1968).

2. Lenski, *Power and Privilege.*

3. It should be obvious, of course, that we have simplified basic principles enumerated by Marx a long time ago. What is remarkable, however, is that Marx assumed them to be suspended at some point in history. A noble vision, but one not supported by historical events. The basic principles of surplus and power are more enduring than Marx would have wished. Gerhard Lenski, in *Power and Privilege*, has made fruitful use of these basic Marxian principles in his historical evolutionary analysis of inequality.

4. This elementary distinction between the study of inequality and the study of stratification has been often obscured. Much of the misunderstanding of the severely criticized Davis–Moore hypothesis, for example, stemmed from the failure to recognize that it was only a theory of how positions were created and why rewards were differentially allocated to positions. The theory—for all its defects—did not address the issue of stratification, of how people move in and out of the positions. Nor did the theory address why they persisted in a particular profile. For relevant commentaries, see: R. Bendix and S. M. Lipset, *Class, Status, and Power,* 2nd ed. (New York: Free Press, 1966), pp. 47–72.

5. There have been a number of good studies focusing, at least in part, on this question. See, for example, S. M. Miller and Pamela Roby, *The Future of Inequality* (New York: Basic Books, 1970); Gabriel Kolko, *Wealth and Power in America* (New York: Praeger, 1962); and Herman Miller, *Rich Man, Poor Man* (New York: Crowell, 1964).

6. Lenski, *Power and Privilege.*

7. Alexis de Tocqueville, *Democracy in America* (New York: Barnes, 1877).

8. For examples of the contemporary radical stance in American sociology, see: David Gordon, *Theories of Poverty and Unemployment* (Lexington, Mass.: Heath-Lexington, 1970); Howard Wachtel, "Looking at Poverty from a Radical Perspective," *Review of Radical Political Economics* 3 (Summer 1971): 1–19; and Pamela Roby, ed., *The Poverty Establishment* (Englewood Cliffs, N.J.: Prentice-Hall, 1974). And of course, the early pioneer work of C. Wright Mills should be acknowledged as the stimulus to the contemporary radical perspective; see in particular, C. Wright Mills, *The Power Elite* (New York: Oxford, 1956); see also the volume

edited by Irving Louis Horowitz on the essays of Mills: *Power, Politics, and People* (New York: Oxford, 1963).

9. Thorstein Veblen, *The Theory of the Leisure Class* (New York: Macmillan, 1899).

10. Gunnar Myrdal, *An American Dilemma* (New York: Harper and Row, 1944).

11. Michael Harrington, *The Other America: Poverty in the United States* (New York: Macmillan, 1963).

2
WEALTH DISTRIBUTION

What is wealth? Wealth can be defined as the total economic assets possessed by people. These assets can be converted to money. Hence, it is possible to visualize such things as cars, equity in homes, stocks, bonds, real estate, and trusts as economic assets: the sum total of all assets possessed by people constituting their *wealth*. The distribution of wealth in a society is one indicator of the degree of overall inequality, because assets that can be converted into money determine access to other scarce resources, such as power, prestige, and health.

As the data on wealth distribution are presented, it is important to recognize that they are incomplete and give only a partial indication of wealth distribution. The incompleteness of wealth data is an interesting political fact that requires analysis. For present purposes, we use what data there are on wealth distribution in America.

CONTINUITIES AND DISCONTINUITIES OF OLD AND NEW WEALTH IN EARLY AMERICA

In some respects the United States is unique among nations in the development of its profile of inequality. Certainly there was continuity between the forms of inequality in the Old World and those in the New World. But the old systems were put under great stress by conditions of international competition and environmental uncertainties in the new and distant land. Many persons undertook their venture to the New World to escape the constrictions of the old class system.[1] Others, however, came as agents of that class system, with the intention of perpetuating old patterns of inequality. Early American wealth was distributed and maintained on essentially the same principles as was wealth in the old countries. The basic differences between the New and Old Worlds were not at the level of the upper class but at the level of the common citizen. Because a great portion of the lower class came to America out of the pauperized masses of Europe, spellbound by the great "get rich" promises of colonial speculators, they held no conventional loyalties to the new industrial class system. The problem of the New World upper class, then, was to create—in a formerly pauperized mass—class loyalty within a relatively open environment that included rich, vast, and unsettled lands and offered a potential escape route from class oppression.

To some extent, a New World landed upper class was inevitable because of the manner in which the colonies were established. Nearly all of the original colonial grants were made directly to already wealthy and powerful Englishmen. Paupers were recruited both as cheap labor for the new lands and to drain off, as the London Company put it, "the fuel of dangerous insurrections" in England. Two joint-stock companies received royal charters to practically all of the land extending two hundred miles inland and from Maine to South Carolina, on condition that they return to King James I one-fifth of all the gold and silver they found. These companies were financed and controlled by some of England's wealthiest merchants. Aided by the lobbying of the Earl of Warwick, a small group of twenty-six men received the grants and charter of the Massachusetts Bay Company. As with other such ventures, the colony and the corporation were virtually identical.

Eventually, these companies were split into others with similar economic arrangements. Maryland was given to Lord Baltimore and remained under the Baltimore family for 144 years. By then, the family's proprietary interests were producing annual income equivalent to $250,000 in 1974. The Carolinas went to eight persons, one of whom was the future Earl of Shaftesbury. To the Duke of York went New York and New Jersey; to William Penn, Pennsylvania. Penn, indeed, received his grant as payoff for a £16,000 (current rate at that time) debt owed to his father by Charles I. His grant gave him control over 55,000 square miles of land.

In addition to these original grants, subsequent grants, contracts, and speculation generated other wealthy landlords. Significant in this respect was the *headright system* by which labor was attracted to the colonies. Under this system, grants of land, usually fifty to one hundred acres, were given for every settler transported to the colonies at the expense of the recipient. Many of the "first families of Virginia" achieved their fortunes this way. Wealthy colonists would find poor persons who were willing to indenture themselves and would transport them to the New World in return for land grants. Under these arrangements some land undoubtedly trickled down to the poor settlers, but most remained in the hands of landlords. For example, the Byrd family of Virginia came to hold over 200,000 acres of land. Robert Carter died in 1722 with an estate of over 300,000 acres. George Washington and a group of fellow speculators received 200,000 acres in the west with a promise of 300,000 more if they would settle one hundred families. In New York, the Van Rensselaers held nearly 700,000 acres, the Van Cortlands 140,000 acres, the Beekmans 240,000 acres, Robert Livingston a tract sixteen miles by twenty-four miles, and a group of speculators, known as the "little nine partners," a grant of 1,000,000 acres.

By the time of the American Revolution, there were many who were as willing to take up arms against the landed gentry of the New World as against King George. Indeed, the years prior to the Revolution had periodically been torn by antirent riots. Although in the end most fought with the revolutionists, there was no doubt a bit of glee expressed when many of the Crown, Loyalist, and proprietary estates were broken up during and after the war. The Tories alone filed claim with the Crown to losses of $40,000,000 in land—although they were eventually granted compensation of only $15,000,000. Sir William Pepperell's Maine holdings had run thirty miles along the coastline; New York's Philipse family holdings contained three hundred square miles; Virginia's Fairfax estate embraced six million acres; and the Penn family claimed $5,000,000 lost. Indeed, it has been estimated that one-half of the state of New York was confiscated from wealthy landlords. Even so, a sizable portion was simply transferred from wealthy Loyalists to wealthy Patriots, such as the Livingston family.

The Revolutionary War may have ended many huge Loyalist fortunes, but it was a war for political independence rather than a social revolution. According to historian Charles Austin Beard, the Constitution was largely a conservative document written by the financiers, businessmen, and speculators of the Patriot upper class. By Beard's calculation, five of every six delegates to the Constitutional Convention stood to gain personally from the new Constitution because of their holdings in securities, businesses, slaves, or land. Conspicuous by their absence were the small farmers, urban laborers, slaves, and radical or potentially radical groups.

The influence of Alexander Hamilton on the new government further evidences the importance of wealth and its control during the first stages of United States history. Hamilton was a central figure in establishing a financial system designed to stabilize the nation under the domination of an Eastern, urban, manufacturing, and moneyed upper class. The beneficiaries of this system were already far from underprivileged. As Hamilton put it to the Constitutional Convention: "(Communities) divide themselves into the few and the many. The first are the rich and well-born, the other the mass of the people . . . turbulent and changing, they seldom judge or determine right. Give therefore to the first class a distinct, permanent share in the Government."[2] The colonies had long followed the English tradition of tying political privilege to property ownership. Even after the Revolution, Massachusetts required wealth of \$300 to vote, \$500 to \$1,000 to run for Congress, \$1,500 to \$3,000 to run for the Senate, and \$5,000 to become governor.

This traditional bias for the wealthy was reflected in many of Hamilton's efforts. When the federal government sought revenues from the sale of western lands, Hamilton was able to make the Land Ordinance of 1785 favor large purchases. Thus, he enhanced the interests of land speculators and eastern manufacturers, protecting the latter from massive loss of cheap labor. His campaign for the Assumption Act, by which the national government assumed state debts, clearly favored Massachusetts and other manufacturing states against southern states and western settlers. In addition, the Assumption Act led to scandalous speculation in securities. Creditors realized enormous windfalls from the interests of debtors, especially former soldiers who had been forced to cash in promissory notes at huge discounts during the depression of 1780. Beneficiaries of the speculation included twenty-nine of the sixty-five members of Congress, three members of President Washington's cabinet, and wealthy arms supplier Robert Morris, "financier of the American Revolution," who personally gained several additional millions. Morris was to gain again as recipient of a bank charter when Hamilton sought to establish a banking system to stabilize credit for the new industrial state he foresaw. Finally, Hamilton joined the new nation to the tradition of tariff politics that give vast indirect subsidies to favored groups while the government picks up funds for administration of other programs. The intent was to aid manufacturing and the factory system. Hamilton had been especially impressed with English factories where employment was "four-sevenths women and children" and the former were "rendered more useful, and the latter more early useful."

We are not suggesting that Hamilton personally created a new economic aristocracy. The process was well underway beforehand and, indeed, the new wealthholders had close ties with the old wealthholders. Our point is that even from the earliest days the United States was neither a land of equality nor a land of equal opportunity. Unfortunately, no historian has yet written a definitive account of inequality as a fundamental force in American history. Beard's analysis of economic forces in the making of the Constitution is only an example of what could be done with the entire political *and* economic development of modern American society. Recent critical studies have begun to tear down the myth of equalitarianism in American history, but they are too incomplete to provide the penetrating, comprehensive account that is needed.

WEALTH INEQUALITY IN THE EARLY UNITED STATES: EVIDENCE ON TWO CITIES

We do consider some of the data on wealth inequality that is becoming available for early periods of the nation's history. We have already cited examples of extreme wealth held during the colonial and revolutionary periods. Such examples serve to define the general range of inequality during that era, especially when that wealth is contrasted with the abject poverty of the mass of citizens and slaves. But these data do not enable us to summarize the relative inequality of wealth through the entire population. To better understand the relative distribution during that period, consider the representative data in Table 1.

Table 1 Distribution of Wealth in America in the 1800s for Selected Cities

Level of Wealth	Percentage of Population in City	Percentage of Total Wealth
(Brooklyn in 1810)		
Under $500	54 ⎱ 66	3 ⎱ 9
$500–1,000	12 ⎰	6 ⎰
$1,000–2,500	20	25
$2,500–4,000	6	11
$4,000–15,000	7 ⎱ 8	33 ⎱ 55
$15,000 or more	1 ⎰	22 ⎰
(Brooklyn in 1841)		
Under $1,000	73	4
$1,000–4,500	15	12
$4,500–15,000	9	24
$15,000–50,000	2	17
$50,000 or more	1	42
(Boston in 1833)		
Under $5,000	86	14
$5,000–30,000	10	27
$30,000–75,000	3	26
$75,000 or more	1	33
(Boston in 1848)		
Under $4,000	81	4
$4,000–35,000	15	32
$35,000–90,000	3	27
$90,000 or more	1	37

Source: Edward Pessen, "The Egalitarian Myth and the American Social Reality: Wealth, Mobility and Equality in the 'Era of the Common Man,'" *American Historical Review* 76, 4(October 1971): 989–1034. Copyright © Edward Pessen.

Table 1 provides a picture of the share of aggregate wealth held by persons of different degrees of wealth for two American cities during the nineteenth century.[3] By comparing the percentage of total wealth held by persons of a given degree of wealthholding with the percentage of the total population they comprise, we can see the concentration of wealth in the hands of the richest citizens. The data provided for these cities cover two points in time and, therefore, provide a rough view of trends in the concentration of wealth in those cities.

The earliest data in the table show that in 1810 the richest 1 percent of the population in Brooklyn owned 22 percent of the total wealth in that city. Those persons each owned *at least* $15,000 wealth (current value in 1810 dollars). When we adjust for differences in the U.S. Department of Labor's consumer price index, we find that this minimum level of wealth among the richest 1 percent was equivalent to $31,915 in 1967 dollars. By contrast with this richest 1 percent, 54 percent of the population of Brooklyn in 1810 owned less than $500 (or $1,064 in 1967 dollars). This poorest portion of the population owned only 3 percent of the total wealth of the city. This comparison makes it obvious that within the city there was an extremely high degree of inequality of wealthholding. The *two* richest classes comprised only 8 percent of the population of the city but held 55 percent of its personally held wealth.

When we turn to the data on wealth distribution in Brooklyn in 1841, thirty-one years later, we find that inequality is just as great if not greater. Although income intervals in the two distributions are not identical and comparisons must be made with additional caution, we can focus on two key contrasts. In the 1810 data, 66 percent of the population owned less than $1,000 and held only 9 percent of the city's wealth. In the 1841 data, 73 percent of the population owned less than $1,000 and held only 4 percent of the city's wealth. Thus, the percentage of those at the bottom appears to have increased while individually and as a group they have become relatively poorer. At the other end of the scale, the wealthiest 1 percent of the city's population were individually wealthier, owning more than $50,000 in 1841 compared to over $15,000 in 1810. In addition, they had almost doubled their share of the city's total private wealth. They had increased their share of holdings from 22 percent to 42 percent of all privately held wealth.

Although the time interval for the Boston data in Table 1 does not correspond exactly to the time interval of the Brooklyn data, it does appear that the trend toward inequality was operative in both cities during the same era. In 1833, 96 percent of the Boston populace owned less than $30,000 and collectively held 41 percent of Boston's privately held wealth. In 1848, 96 percent of Boston's population owned less than $35,000 and collectively held 36 percent of the privately held wealth. The richest 4 percent of the population of Boston increased its share of the wealth from 59 percent in 1833 to 64 percent in 1848, and nearly all of this increase went to the very richest 1 percent of citizens.

In analyzing inequality in any society or group, we are forced into decisions about how to present data and what data are relevant to the specific questions we may want to ask. For example, we may wish to know how wealthy the richest people are, how poor the poorest. Or, we may wish to know how much wealth is held by specific social groups or by persons of given demographic characteristics. These are essentially scale questions. They pertain to the location of persons along the scale by which the society or social group counts its wealth. Scale questions may be asked about individuals or about classes. Questions asked about individuals raise the additional matter of how persons are to be classified. Do we define narrow or broad wealth classes? Do we define classes statistically or by popular or professional sociological labeling systems?

There are only a limited number of significant distributional questions that can be asked about either real or hypothetical *individuals*. Questions about wealth inequality among real individuals are of little analytic value except in highly constricted theories about very small groups. These questions cannot take us far in our search for understanding the structure and dynamic of inequality in the larger society. For such understanding, we must begin with classes, families, or other groups and ascertain their shares of wealth.

Populations may increase or decrease in size, become richer or poorer, and alter their distribution of wealth toward more or less inequality. Similarly, when comparing two or more populations, we may find differences in their sizes, their levels of total wealth, and their degrees of inequality. In consequence, comparative statistics require some standardization to reduce the risks of spurious conclusions. The conventional method for removing the effects of different population sizes or different levels of total wealth is to convert amounts of wealth held into percentages and, similarly, to convert the size of relevant subpopulations into percentages of the total population.

Under the condition of perfect equality of wealth, the wealth of each subpopulation would constitute a percentage of the total wealth identical to its percentage of the total population. For example, any group comprising 1 percent of the population would, under perfect wealth equality, possess *exactly* 1 percent of total wealth. A group is less favored than it would be under strict egalitarianism if its percentage share of wealth is less than its percentage share of population. A group is more privileged than it would be under strict egalitarianism if its percentage share of wealth is greater than its percentage share of population. This corollary of strict equality suggests a common solution to the problem of classification of individuals for purposes of analyzing the degree and pattern of inequality in any given society. The solution consists of forming *statistical* classes and calculating what economists call the *size distribution* of wealth or, in simpler terms, the percentage of the total wealth.

The data of Table 1 are presented as size distributions. Each distribution in the table takes a given population for a city and defines *ordered* classes according to the magnitude of wealth held by this statistical class. For each ordered class, the number of persons in that class is stated as a percentage of the total population, and the aggregate wealth they hold is stated as a percentage of the total private wealth held by all persons in the entire population. By comparing these percentages within wealth classes, we can ascertain the advantage or disadvantage of each class relative to the state of equality. By comparing the percentages across wealth classes, we can gauge the degree of concentration of wealth among the richer and poorer segments of the population.

Nevertheless, some size distributions are more effective displays, for analytic purposes, than others. The amount of wealth held by persons in any interval of wealth depends on both the levels of wealth in the interval and the number of persons at those levels. By shifting the number and width of wealth intervals in a distribution, the analyst can impose virtually any apparent pattern. It is, therefore, necessary to adopt some restraints. The conventional restraint is to present self-ordered size distributions wherein interval limits are chosen so that all classes have *the same proportion of the total population.*

Where possible we adopt the most common solution to this problem, which is to present size distributions in *ordered fifths* of population. The population is divided into five equal groups (20 percent of the total population) and each group's respective share of the total wealth is then determined. Such distributions are given in the lower section of Table 2 for three additional American cities in mid-nineteenth century. The advantage of such distributions over those for Brooklyn and Boston is their standard format. This format allows direct comparison over time and place throughout the full distributions.[4]

Table 2 The Distribution of Wealth in America for Selected Cities

Level of Wealth	Percentage of Population	Percentage of Wealth Held in 1860 in:		
		Baltimore	New Orleans	St. Louis
Highest fifth	20	94.7	92.9	92.7
Second fifth	20	4.4	5.7	6.0
Middle fifth	20	0.9	1.3	1.1
Fourth fifth	20	0.0	0.0	0.2
Poorest fifth	20	0.0	0.0	0.0

Source: Robert E. Gallman, "Trends in the Size Distribution of Wealth in the Nineteenth Century: Some Speculation," in *Six Papers on the Size Distribution of Wealth and Income,* ed. Lee Soltow (New York: National Bureau of Economic Research and Columbia University Press, 1969), pp. 1–25.

The data for Baltimore, New Orleans, and St. Louis present consistent patterns of inequality of wealth. In each city, the richest 20 percent of the population possessed over 90 percent of the privately held wealth, and the poorest 20 percent possessed none. Indeed, for all practical accounts, we suggest that 40 percent of the population of those cities held all of the wealth.

Although the data for Baltimore, New Orleans, and St. Louis follow nineteen and twelve years after our latest data for Brooklyn and Boston, respectively, there is a basic consistency among all distributions. The Boston data for 1848 show virtually the same concentration of wealth in the top 20 percent—19 percent of the Bostonians held 96 percent of the wealth. The Brooklyn data for 1841 illustrate the difficulties of making comparisons when self-ordered distributions are not used, because we have no way of ascertaining the proportion of wealth held by the top 20 percent of wealthholders. Still, since the top 27 percent are shown to have held 96 percent of wealth, we can be sure that Brooklyn's pattern of inequality was essentially similar to the patterns of the other cities.

The size distributions for Brooklyn and Boston are helpful in showing *how much* wealthier the rich were relative to the poor. The size distributions for Baltimore, New Orleans, and St. Louis are most useful for revealing the comparative concentration of wealth over the various populations. In either case, however, it is obvious that American cities in the early to mid-nineteenth century were characterized by gross inequality of wealth. The evidence raises considerable doubt about the long-standing myth of American egalitarianism. In particular, it undermines the myth of the middle class canonized by de Tocqueville and other chroniclers of the era.

TRENDS IN TWENTIETH CENTURY CONCENTRATION OF WEALTH

In some respects, the conventional size distributions in quintiles conceal the extreme concentration at the top. When so great a share of wealth is held by the richest 20 percent of the population, much of the pattern of wealthholding is collapsed into a single interval and the internal variability is obscured. For this reason, many scholars provide a supplementary subinterval for the wealthiest 5 percent or for the wealthiest 1 percent of the population. In Table 3 we present a continuation of historical evidence on the concentration of wealth in the United States. Table 3 gives data collected from several sources on the percentage share

Table 3 Share of Wealth Held by Richest 1 Percent, United States

Year	Percentage of Wealth Held	By 1 Percent of:
1810	21.0	U.S. families
1860	24.0	U.S. families
1900	26.0–31.0	U.S. families
1922	31.6	U.S. adults
1929	36.3	U.S. adults
1933	28.3	U.S. adults
1939	30.6	U.S. adults
1945	23.3	U.S. adults
1949	20.8	U.S. adults
1953	27.5	U.S. adults
1956	26.0	U.S. adults
1958	26.9	U.S. adults
1962	27.4	U.S. adults
1965	29.2	U.S. adults
1969	24.9	U.S. adults

Sources: For 1810, 1860, and 1900, Robert E. Gallman, "Trends in the Size Distribution of Wealth in the Nineteenth Century," in *Six Papers on the Size Distribution of Wealth and Income*, ed. Lee Soltow (New York: National Bureau of Economic Research, 1969), p. 6.

For 1922, 1929, 1933, 1939, 1945, 1949, and 1956, Robert J. Lampman, *The Share of Top Wealthholders in National Wealth 1922–1956* (New York: National Bureau of Economic Research, 1962), p. 204.

For 1953, 1958, 1962, 1965, and 1969, James D. Smith and Stephen D. Franklin, "The Concentration of Personal Wealth, 1922–1969," *American Economic Review* 64, 2 (May 1974): 162–167, at p. 166.

Note: Smith and Franklin report that data for 1962, 1965, and 1969 were adjusted to achieve statistical comparability with the earlier 1953 and 1958 data. The result sacrifices their best estimates for the later years in the interest of consistency and, they note, produces a downward bias in their best estimates of wealth concentration. The bias is estimated to be 10 to 15 percent. Thus, the actual concentration of wealth in the years 1962, 1965, and 1969 could run as high as 32.2 percent, 34.8 percent, and 29.8 percent, respectively.

of total private wealth held by the wealthiest 1 percent of American families or adults.

The wealthiest 1 percent has held a share of wealth ranging from roughly 21 to 32 percent of all wealth. This share of about 25 percent has been rather consistent from 1810 to the present. Although the 1810 share recorded in Table 3 is almost identical to the 1810 share of the wealthiest 1 percent of Brooklyn (Table 1), the 1860 share belies the markedly higher concentrations in the data for Boston in 1833 and 1848 and for Brooklyn in 1841. Nevertheless, there does appear to have been an increasing concentration of wealth up to the beginning of World War II. Since World War II, there seems to have been a slight decrease in the share of total wealth held by the richest 1 percent of adults. Unfortunately, long-term data are not available for assessing trends throughout the full range of wealthholding. We are unable to determine shifts that may have taken place among classes of less wealth. This is partly a consequence of the relation of wealth to power and partly a result of the late development of statistics.

The deliberate production of statistical archives for purposes of systematic regulation of social and economic affairs and for the guidance of public policy is of recent origin. The tools of statistical analysis have been developed during the twentieth century, as has the motivation for their use in policy studies and societal monitoring. Largely as a result of the massive growth of the federal government during the Great Depression, World War II, and the Cold War, we are now beginning to acquire secondary data that form the basis for understanding the wealth structure of the United States. We are still dependent on data acquired for other purposes. And access to those data is restricted by the general reluctance of public agencies to collect such information or to release it. For all practical purposes, the available evidence on personal wealthholding is of two types. The classical type is data on the financial characteristics of consumers—collected primarily as a service to business and the federal government. The second type is tax-related data from the Internal Revenue Service. The Bureau of the Census, which provides most of our data on current income and a plethora of other matters, has never been a major source for data on wealth. This situation is suggestive of the political economics of wealth.

Among the data on financial characteristics of consumers is a study released by the Board of Governors of the Federal Reserve. This exceptional study contains detailed information on wealthholding. Despite its hearty reception, no governmental agency has ever replicated it. Perhaps the revelations it contained were too threatening to the egalitarian myth. However, the data provide a good description of the contemporary structure of wealth inequality in the United States in 1962.

Table 4 shows the percentage of consumer units that, in 1962, fell within each of several money classes when judged by either of two measures. In the first instance, consumer units are placed in *wealth* classes derived by subtracting from the 1962 market value of their assets all debts which they held by virtue of secured loans. Among the 57.9 million consumer units—families, and persons not in families—5.7 million units, or roughly 10 percent, held zero or negative wealth. At the same time, some 3.9 million consumer units, or roughly 6 percent of all units, held unencumbered wealth valued at $50,000 or more. Table 4 also provides a distribution of consumer units by net worth. *Net worth* refers to the market value of wealth reduced by the value of all debts not secured by assets. Because many poor persons have negligible assets or none, unsecured debts may be common among them. Such debts, in effect, place a lien on the peoples' lives rather than their properties—or, less dramatically, a lien on their labor.

When net worth is the basis of placing consumer units into money classes, the effect is to sharply inflate the percentage of units at the poorer levels while leaving the percentage at richer levels virtually unchanged. When net worth is our measure, we find that the units in the zero or negative money classes have risen to 16 percent of the total. The general effect of choosing net worth over wealth (unencumbered assets) appears to be to shift some units in classes below $10,000 further downward in the distribution. The severity of the impact of taking into account unsecured debts suggests that net worth is a more accurate measure of the well-being of many poorer people than is the wealth or equity measure. Nevertheless, the bulk of data released under this study pertain to the notion of wealth as asset equity.

Table 4 Distribution of Consumer Units (Families and Individuals) by Wealth[a] and Net Worth,[b] 1962

Money Class	Percentage of Consumer Units, by:		Mean Wealth of Wealth Class
	Wealth Class	*Net Worth Class*	
$ Negative	2	11	——
$ Zero	8	5	——
$1–999	16	12	$ 396
$1,000–4,999	19	17	2,721
$5,000–9,999	16	15	7,267
$10,000–24,999	23	23	16,047
$25,000–49,999	11	10	35,191
$50,000–99,999	4	4	68,980
$100,000–199,999	1	1	132,790
$200,000–499,999	1	1	300,355
$500,000 and Over	c	1	1,260,667
Total	101[d]	100	$ 20,982

Source: Dorothy S. Projector and Gertrude S. Weiss, *Survey of Financial Characteristics of Consumers,* Federal Reserve Technical Papers (Washington, D.C.: Federal Reserve Board, August 1966), Tables A1 and A2, pp. 96–99.

[a]Wealth is defined as assets minus asset-secured debts.

[b]Net Worth is defined as wealth minus unsecured debts.

[c]Less than 1 percent.

[d]Does not add to 100 percent because of rounding.

A further indication of the structure of wealthholding in 1962 is the array of mean value of wealth held by each wealth class. Persons in the negative wealth class have debts well in excess of assets, and those in the zero wealth class are probably in debt by virtue of unsecured loans. In column three of Table 4, we see that the 16 percent of consumer units in the first wealth class with unencumbered assets have a mean wealth, not counting unsecured debts, of only $396. Thus, 26 percent of consumer units in 1962 had clear assets of less than $1,000 and with mean value less than $400. At the other extreme, the 200,000 consumer units, less than 1 percent of all units, with the greatest wealth held at least $500,000 and averaged out at well above $1,250,000. Put another way, it would take roughly 3,184 units in the lowest *"solvent"* wealth class to collectively equal the wealth of the average consumer unit in the wealthiest class. And that ignores the huge mass of consumer units that are insolvent.

Because most Americans live in family units, families are the primary referent by which most Americans evaluate their well-being. The data we have been discussing, however, refer to consumer units. Consumer units include both families and individuals not in families. In Table 5, we present size distributions for net worth of families. As this table shows, 8.1 percent of families have *negative* net worth equivalent to 0.2 percent of total national net worth. This negative worth exactly balances the 0.2 percent of real net worth of the 17.3 percent of families with net worth of zero to $1,000. This shows up in the cumulative percentage distribution. There we see that the poorest 25.4 percent of families, measured by net worth, have 0.0 percent of the total net worth. This finding is reminiscent of the 1860 data from Baltimore, New Orleans, and St. Louis in Table 2, where we found that at least 20 percent of persons in those cities shared in none of the privately held wealth. On the other hand, the top 20 percent of persons in those cities held over 90 percent of the wealth. For our 1962 families, Table 5 suggests that

Table 5 Distribution of Net Worth (Assets Less Debt), United States Families, 1962

Net Worth (thousands of dollars)	Percentages of:		Cumulative Percentages of:	
	Families	Net Worth	Families	Net Worth
Negative	8.1	− 0.2	8.1	− 0.2
0–1	17.3	0.2	25.4	0.0
1–5	17.3	2.1	42.7	2.1
5–10	14.2	4.5	56.9	6.6
10–25	24.4	17.2	81.3	23.8
25–50	11.2	17.1	92.5	40.9
50–100	5.1	15.0	97.6	55.9
100–200	1.0	5.4	98.6	61.3
200–500	0.9	12.9	99.5	74.2
500 and Over	0.5	25.8	100.0	100.0

Source: Lester B. Thurow and Robert E. B. Lucas, *The American Distribution of Income: A Structural Problem*, a study prepared for the use of the Joint Economic Committee, 92nd Congress (Washington, D.C.: Government Printing Office, 1972), Table 7, page 12.

wealth may not be quite as concentrated at the top. Those with net wealth above $25,000 comprised 18.7 percent of all families and held 76.2 percent of the net worth of families in the United States. Despite the apparent, century-long decline in the share of the top 20 percent, one can scarcely deny or applaud the continued concentration of wealth in the hands of the very wealthy. Families with net worth over $500,000 possess a munificent 25.8 percent of total family net worth, although they constitute merely 0.5 percent of all families.

Fortunately, the U.S. Department of Commerce has provided size distributions self-ordered by fifths of consumer units for the 1962 Federal Reserve data. Three separate distributions are given in Table 6 and Figure 1 under different modes of ordering the fifths of consumer units. When units are ordered by level of wealth, we see that the top 40 percent of units held 91.5 percent of all wealth, with the top 20 percent holding 76.0 percent. In contrast, the bottom 40 percent held only 2.1 percent of total wealth, and the bottom 20 percent held a mere 0.2 percent. Despite the myth of the great American middle class, the middle 60 percent of consumer units held only 23.8 percent of the total private wealth. Nor does the myth fare appreciably better when we order fifths of consumer units by current annual income. The 60 percent of consumer units in the middle of the income range held only 35.6 percent of all privately held wealth. The highest 20 percent of income earners held 57.2 percent of private wealth; the poorest 20 percent held 7.2 percent of private wealth. Finally, we see that fifths of consumer units ordered by age of head show somewhat less inequality of wealth. Evidently, the heavy concentration of wealth in the highest wealth and income fifths is not primarily due to career accumulation of fortunes. At least, not every career ends in such happy circumstances. While the richest 20 percent own 76.0 percent of wealth, the oldest 60 percent own 79 percent. It follows that wealth becomes concentrated well before retirement time.

Table 6 Distribution of Wealth: 1962

Percentage of Total Wealth Held by Fifths of Units					
By Size of Wealth		By Income		By Age of Head	
Fifths of Units	Percent of Total Wealth	Fifths of Units	Percent of Total Wealth	Fifths of Units	Percent of Total Wealth
Total	100.0	Total	100.0	Total	100.0
Lowest fifth	.2	Lowest fifth	7.2	Youngest fifth	6.0
Second fifth	2.1	Second fifth	8.6	Second fifth	14.3
Middle fifth	6.2	Middle fifth	11.4	Middle fifth	20.7
Fourth fifth	15.5	Fourth fifth	15.6	Fourth fifth	29.2
Highest fifth	76.0	Highest fifth	57.2	Oldest fifth	29.8

Source: Board of Governors of the Federal Reserve System, "Survey of Financial Characteristics of Consumers, 1962, as reported in the Department of Commerce's *Social Indicators, 1973* (Washington, D.C.: Government Printing Office, 1973).

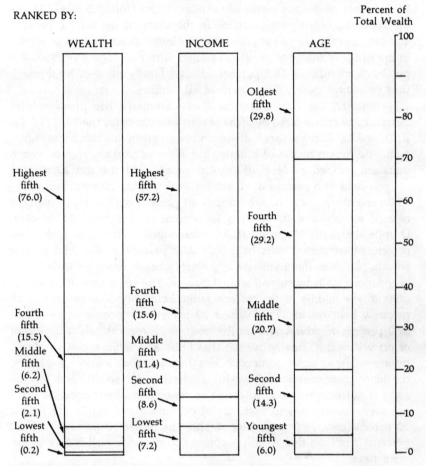

Figure 1 Distribution of Wealth: 1962
Fifths of Consumer Units Ranked by Wealth, Income, and Age

RANKED BY:

Percent of Total Wealth

WEALTH   INCOME   AGE

WEALTH:
Highest fifth (76.0)
Fourth fifth (15.5)
Middle fifth (6.2)
Second fifth (2.1)
Lowest fifth (0.2)

INCOME:
Highest fifth (57.2)
Fourth fifth (15.6)
Middle fifth (11.4)
Second fifth (8.6)
Lowest fifth (7.2)

AGE:
Oldest fifth (29.8)
Fourth fifth (29.2)
Middle fifth (20.7)
Second fifth (14.3)
Youngest fifth (6.0)

Source: Executive Office of the President: Office of Management and Budget, *Social Indicators 1973* (Washington, D.C.: Government Printing Office, 1973), p. 164.

The size distributions given above clearly establish that a gross pattern of inequality in wealth existed among consumer units in 1962. From this fundamental fact, we now turn to consider the composition of wealthholding for the various wealth classes. Unfortunately we cannot give the full picture because many of the available data bypass the debtor classes we found at the bottom of the pyramid of wealth. The omission of negative and zero wealthholding classes is a commentary on the limited perspectives and purposes of those who have had direct access to the raw data.[5] Perhaps business and governmental agencies and their academic associates see no profit in debt. In most cases we must infer the status of zero and negative wealthholders from slight differences between figures for all consumer units and the general pattern for specific wealth classes given in the tables. In other words, we extrapolate trends that appear as we move from the richer to the poorer wealth classes and use the figures for all units as a check.

FROM DEBTOR TO SUPERWEALTHY: PATTERNS OF WEALTHHOLDING

Wealth has been defined as asset equity. Hence, we can ask what kinds of assets provide the wealth of units at each level of wealth. To ascertain this, assets have been grouped into six types: home, auto, business or profession, cash or savings, investments, and miscellaneous. Cash and savings are termed *liquid* assets because of their ready availability for expenditures. Investment assets are primarily composed of marketable securities, speculative real estate, and mortgages. Miscellaneous assets are, in the aggregate, dominated by beneficial interests in trusts.

Table 7 Percentage of Consumer Units Who Have Some Equity in Specific Assets, by Wealth Size, December 31, 1962

			Asset Type			
Wealth[a] Size	Home[b] (percent)	Auto-mobile (percent)	Business and profession[c] (percent)	Liquid assets[d] (percent)	Invest-ment Assets[e] (percent)	Miscel-laneous Assets[f] (percent)
All Units:[g]	57	73	17	79	31	8
$1–999	9	74	3	70	4	3
$1,000–4,999	54	76	8	78	14	6
$5,000–9,999	78	77	16	85	30	7
$10,000–24,999	84	82	19	96	42	11
$25,000–49,999	80	88	38	97	64	15
$50,000–99,999	72	89	54	98	89	15
$100,000–199,999	86	93	53	100	93	16
$200,000–499,999	84	84	57	97	95	12
$500,000 and over	81	79	66	100	99	52

Source: Dorothy S. Projector and Gertrude S. Weiss, *Survey of Financial Characteristics of Consumers* (Washington, D.C.: Board of Governors of the Federal Reserve System, August 1966), p. 110.

[a]Wealth: equity in named assets.

[b]Own home: principal residence and vacation homes.

[c]Business and profession: equities in family owned and operated businesses, professional practices, and farms.

[d]Liquid assets: checking accounts, savings, and United States savings bonds.

[e]Investment assets: marketable securities, investment real estate, and mortgages.

[f]Miscellaneous assets: largely assets held in personal trusts.

[g]Consumer unit: families and unrelated individuals as defined by the Bureau of the Census.

As a benchmark, we first consider the holdings of all consumer units of the 1962 survey (including debtor units). From Table 7 we see that 79 percent of all units had some liquid assets and 73 percent had some equity in autos. These asset forms, therefore, appear to be the most commonly used forms of wealth. Home equity was the only other form of asset held by a majority of consumer units. Relatively fewer units held assets in the form of investments, equity in a business or profession, or in miscellaneous forms.

In addition to knowing the proportion of consumer units having *some* equity in assets of given types, it is important to consider the average value of assets of each type when they are held. Table A1 of the appendix to this chapter provides this information. The table gives the mean value of holdings by asset type for all consumer units of the 1962 survey and for all such units according to their wealth class.

From Table A1 we learn that the mean wealth of all consumer units in the 1962 survey was $20,982. However, we know from our earlier size distributions that 60 percent of all these consumer units fell below the $10,000 level of wealthholding. Thus, we know that the mean wealth of nearly $21,000 is a misleading guide to the wealth of the typical consumer unit. Still, we can ask for the value of specific asset holdings that go into this average. When we do so, we find that the largest component is a mean of roughly $7,000 in investments. This is followed by a mean equity of $5,653 in housing, $3,881 in business or profession assets, $2,675 in liquid assets, $1,116 in miscellaneous assets, and only $644 in auto equity.

When we switch from composition in terms of the percent of units possessing some equity of given types to the mean value of equity in those types, the great American golden egg—the auto—turns out to be a lead pellet. We all depend on it. Indeed, the economy has become dependent on it. It forms the first element in the search for economic security (and ostentation) but ends as a negligible factor in the securing of wealth.

In terms of mean value, investment assets contributed the most to the gross average wealth of all consumer units, although only 31 percent of consumer units possessed any investment assets at all. Whereas investment assets were fourth most common among types of asset holdings, they were of first importance in average contribution of gross mean wealth. This exactly reverses the situation that held with respect to liquid assets. Housing equity, however, remains in the middle of the thicket under either way of looking at the distribution of wealth. These features are collectively suggestive of and reflect the ways in which wealth inequality develops and is maintained.

By looking at the mean value of specific asset holdings as a percentage of the mean value of all asset types together, we can gauge the relative significance of asset types for all consumer units and within wealth levels. Table 8 provides this information for consumer units in the 1962 survey.

The mean value of wealth in investments constituted 33.4 percent of the mean value of all wealth for all consumer units. Home equity added another 26.9 percent to take second place in importance of contribution to mean value of wealth. Assets in business or profession contributed 18.4 percent; liquid assets contributed 12.7 percent; miscel-

Table 8 Mean Value of Assets of Specific Types As Percentage of Mean Value of
Wealth of All Types by Wealth Class of Consumer Units, 1962

Wealth Class	Total (percent)	Asset Type					
		Home	Auto-mobile	Business or Profession	Liquid	Invest-ments	Miscel-laneous
All Units	100	26.9	3.1	18.4	12.7	33.4	5.3
$1–999	100	10.1	48.0	2.3	33.8	3.5	2.3
$1,000–4,999	100	47.7	16.4	3.0	25.8	6.2	0.9
$5,000–9,999	100	58.6	8.4	8.6	16.9	6.1	1.4
$10,000–24,999	100	55.1	5.3	9.3	16.3	12.7	1.0
$25,000–49,999	100	36.9	3.2	18.8	18.1	21.3	1.5
$50,000–99,999	100	20.5	2.2	24.2	15.7	35.5	1.7
$100,000–199,999	100	17.2	1.7	17.3	14.2	48.3	1.4
$200,000–499,999	100	8.6	0.8	24.1	7.0	56.3	3.2
$500,000 and over	100	4.5	0.2	23.4	3.7	49.8	18.4

Source: Dorothy S. Projector and Gertrude S. Weiss, *Survey of Financial Characteristics of Consumers* (Washington, D.C.: Board of Governors of the Federal Reserve System, August 1966), p. 110.

laneous assets provided 5.3 percent; and auto equity filled in the remainder with 3.1 percent of mean value of wealth.

We begin to see the changing role of various assets when we compare the composition of wealth at various levels. When we step above the ranks of those who had negative or zero wealth to the first class with any positive wealth, those with $1 to $999, auto equity and liquid assets were practically the only types these units were likely to hold. The trend of wealth composition over wealth levels also suggests that that was even more true of the excluded zero and negative wealth classes. It appears that all such underclass persons could hope for in the collective grab for wealth was a few bucks worth of a tin Lizzy and a little grocery money. The value of these two factors, on the average, for persons in the $1 to $999 class, was $190 and $134, respectively. Auto and liquid assets comprised 81.8 percent of the wealth of these consumers. Doubtless the omitted debtors found it even tougher to acquire financial security.

By contrast, those in the top wealth class held an average wealth of $1,260,667. They appear to have been especially fond of investment assets, which they held to the tune of an average of $628,271 and which composed 49.8 percent of their mean wealth. Along with business and profession assets, which are close functional relatives of investment assets, investment wealth constituted 73.2 percent of the mean wealth of the top wealth class. And, if we add their miscellaneous assets of $232,356, 95.8 percent of which was in the form of beneficial interests in trusts (a favorite strongbox of the rich), we find that 91.6 percent of their wealth could be attributed to equity in trusts, businesses, or investments. The staples of poor people's wealth—homes, liquid assets, and autos—fade to near insignificance in the wealth of the superrich. At the bottom of *their* list was the auto, which accounted for only 0.2 percent of their mean wealth and contributed only $2,679. Still, $2,679 was nearly seven times the *total* mean wealth of the poorest wealth-holders—not to mention those who had none.

Nor are the embryonic superrich of the next lower wealth class very different. Those units held between $200,000 and $500,000, with mean holdings of $300,355. Although their average holdings were less than one-fourth the holdings of those over $500,000, their investment holdings were even more important to them. Investment holdings provided 56.3 percent of their average wealth; business and profession assets added another 24.1 percent. One might say that the crucial difference between the top class and the next most wealthy class, to interpolate F. Scott Fitzgerald, is that the former have more money. But there are some further differences even here. We see in the top wealth class a tremendous jump in the value and importance of beneficial interests in trust funds. Only in the top wealth class of the 1962 data did more than 16 percent of consumer units hold miscellaneous assets beyond the basic five we have discussed. In the top wealth class, the corresponding percentage jumped to 54 percent. Further, the value of miscellaneous assets remained fairly low until the next to top wealth class, and even then comprised only 3.2 percent of the mean wealth of that group. But that is only part of the story, for such facts obscure the point that trust funds explode onto the scene only at the top wealth level. Fully 26 percent of consumer units at the top wealth level held beneficial interests in trusts; this compares with the 4 percent who held such interests at the next lower wealth level and the even smaller percentages below that. Further, at the top wealth level, consumer units held an average[6] value in trust wealth of $222,600, while at the next lower level the comparable figure was $5,393. At the top wealth level, trust funds comprised 95.8 percent of all miscellaneous assets. For perspective on the emergence at the top of trust funds to protect wealth, we refer the reader to Table A2 of the Appendix, which gives the distribution of trust interests over the wealth classes.

We shall have more to say about the role of trust funds in the creation and maintenance of wealth. Here, however, we return to the discussion of differences in wealthholdings at the various levels of wealth. As previously noted, liquid assets and auto equity were held to some degree by the vast majority of all consumer units with some wealth. Nevertheless, the likelihood of holding such forms of wealth increased, with one minor exception, as wealth level increased. The minor exception is that likelihood of an auto equity peaked in the $100,000 to $199,999 wealth class and declined above that. We can speculate that this merely reflects the ability of the superwealthy to purchase planes or to substitute other, more favored modes of transportation. The significance of the auto as a component of wealth declines with especial rapidity as we move upward through the ranks of wealth. Liquid assets experienced a similar but less rapid decline in significance, although they contributed over 10 percent of mean wealth until the level of $200,000 and above.

Home equity was held by only 9 percent of consumer units with $1 to $999 of total wealth and constituted but 10.1 percent of their mean wealth. When we move to the next level, however, where wealth averaged $2,721 rather than the $396 of the first level, 54 percent of consumer units had some home equity. The mean value of their home equity was $1,298 or 47.7 percent of their total mean wealth. At this wealth level, home, auto, and liquid assets formed 89.9 percent of mean total wealth. Home equity was even more important in the composition of the wealthholdings of those at the $5,000 to $9,999 and the $10,000 to $24,999 levels of wealthholding.

From the trends in wealthholding and wealth composition, we can offer a rough view of the way social classes in America are related to property differences. The ladder of wealth appears, as could be expected, to begin with liquid assets—probably of the cash or checking account variety. Hardly separable is the first elementary holding of equity in automobiles. Jobs and cars go together in American society, whether we speak of problems of persons or industrial dependencies. Without transportation many people could not obtain or hold jobs. But, jobs are necessary to purchase transportation. Many poor people *ad hoc* their way along until they can purchase the independence of movement that a car can bring. No wonder that the first goal of many youngsters entering the labor market is to get that down payment on a set of wheels. As we have seen, auto equity and some liquid assets are the only assets held by a substantial percentage of those at the bottom of the pyramid of wealth. While these assets loom large in the wealth of these people, we should remember that their wealth is very meager.

Those who possessed $1,000 to $4,999 in the 1962 survey rested at the edge of the second rung of property building. This was the first group in which a majority of consumer units hold equity in homes. Their holdings of home equity accounted for 54 percent of the increase in mean wealth over that of the next lower level, an increase in value of $2,325. Indeed, whereas auto equity had formed the major portion of the meager average wealth below this level, home equity now became dominant. This confirms what most of us know from our own struggles to get ahead in the game of economic security and well-being. Young families turn from concern with getting a job and a car to finding a home of their own. But since 26 percent of consumer units in the 1962 survey fell below the level of wealth in which homeowning became meaningful, we surmise that many do not find their dream house. Or, if they find it, the best they can do is rent it.

Three intervals in the 1962 wealth distribution appear to be characterized by the dominance of homeownership in the wealth of consumer units. The level just mentioned, $1,000 to $4,999, is at the bottom of a broad middle band of wealth. The second level in this band runs from $5,000 to $9,999 and could be viewed as the defining level. In it 58.6 percent of mean wealth could be attributed to home equity. Auto equity began to rapidly fade to insignificance as a factor in mean wealth, and liquid assets dropped sharply to a lower plateau. The upper level of the middle band—$10,000 to $24,999—suggests the emergence of a higher property class. The middle band of three intervals runs from $1,000 to $24,999 and covers 58 percent of all consumer units. One is tempted to say that this middle band typifies the middle class in American society. It is not at all homogeneous, as the levels show, but the fact that roughly half or more of the mean wealth of these units is tied up in homeownership gives it a characteristic feature. This feature often gives the members of this middle band a social identity and solidarity that overrides internal conflicts of interest and emerges as a potent political force. Too often, however, this force is exercised against the large minority of units at the bottom rather than against those at the pinnacle.

When we leave the levels of wealth below $25,000 in the 1962 data, we approach the kingdom of the giants. At the first steps into this kingdom we encounter the gatekeepers with wealth of $25,000 to $49,999. They held average wealth of $35,191, more than twice the average wealth of those in the $10,000 to $24,999 interval. But what really distinguished them from their underlings was the sharp decline in the portion of their wealth due to home equity and a simultaneous jump in the contributions of two new forms of property. Home equity dropped from 55.1 percent of mean wealth to 36.9 percent. But, equity in a business or profession suddenly doubled as it rose to 18.8 percent of mean wealth for the interval. Similarly, investment assets sharply increased to 21.3 percent of the interval's mean wealth. Businesses, professions, investments—these are the great concerns of the capitalist elite. And they define the property class at the peak of the wealth pyramid.

Above the $25,000 mark, home equity rapidly declined in significance. Equity in a business or profession reached a stable plateau of roughly 18 percent to 24 percent of mean wealth. Investment assets, on the other hand, rapidly rose in significance and comprised an increasing portion of mean wealth. Above $100,000, investments were approximately 50 percent of mean wealth. Recalling that investment assets are largely in the form of ownership of corporate stock, real estate, and mortgages, we see that ownership of the means of production defines the property base of the dominant wealth class of the United States. Ownership of the means of production, as indicated by percentage of wealth in investment assets and equity in a business or profession, comprised 59.7 percent, 65.6 percent, 80.4 percent, and 73.2 percent of mean wealth over the top four intervals, respectively. If we regard the monetary value of beneficial trusts for the superwealthy as a *covert* form of capitalist ownership, then the centrality of this property form at the top of the wealth pyramid is even more evident. Thus, capitalist wealth comprised 61.4 percent, 67.0 percent, 83.6 percent, and 91.6 percent, respectively, of the wealth of the four wealth intervals beginning at $50,000.

Members of the $25,000 to $49,999 interval were but the gatekeepers to this estate class. They still held traces of kinship with the class characterized by homeownership. Home equity had not yet been eclipsed in value by either investment assets or assets in a business or profession, although it had been surpassed by the two together.

Above the $50,000 mark we are in the estate class. Here mean wealth ran higher than the $60,000 which even the United States government recognizes as defining the estate class. Thus, wealth at that level is considered of such magnitude as to warrant a tax on wealth. But, of course, wealth carries power, and the official recognition of the estate class is mostly a matter of implicit principle. The tax on wealth which it generates is not applied until the wealthholder dies. Even then various legal devices are available for evading portions of the tax. Indeed, one of the favorite devices is the beneficial trust, which we note emerges as a significant form of wealth for those at the very peak of the wealth pyramid. By placing sizable portions of their wealth in generation-skipping trusts, the very wealthy frequently escape, or lower, estate and inheritance taxes. But this is only one weapon they use in a war for wealth that dwarfs the so-called public war on poverty canonized in the sixties.

Whether one takes the size distribution of wealth as evidence of the wealthy's success in the war for wealth or as evidence of the power base from which they fight, there can be little doubt about the extreme contrast between the conditions of the rich and those of the poor. The heavy concentration of wealth at the top has already been displayed. It is, however, instructive to view the matter in terms of the size distributions of specific forms of wealth. To complete our discussion of the 1962 Federal Reserve study, we have reproduced size distributions for the various asset types in Table 9.

Viewed from this perspective, the comparative property bases of wealthholders become more apparent. A rough order exists in the overlapping of property types as intervals increase in wealth: autos, homes, liquid assets, real estate, mortgage assets, directly managed business or profession, business not managed by the unit, publicly traded stocks, other marketable securities, and miscellaneous (trust) assets.

This order may be inferred by proceeding as follows. First, we collapse the $100,000 to $199,999 and the $200,000 to $499,999 intervals into one interval. This step is taken, after close inspection of adjacent intervals to insure that no major distortion of trends is produced, to provide more continuity between intervals. After this step, we successively identify those intervals holding 20 percent, 15 percent, or 10 percent of the wealth in each asset type. Within each asset type, we note the effect of choosing among these criteria in deciding which are the dominant intervals of wealthholders. This presents the patterns shown in Table 10.

From these patterns, some things are evident. Most important is the essential absence of any of the poorest four intervals among those classes

Table 9 Percentage Share of Total Wealth, Consumer Units, and Wealth in Specific Assets by Wealth Size, 1962 Consumer Units

Wealth Size	Consumer Units	Total Wealth	Home Assets	Auto Assets	Business Profession Assets	Liquid Assets	Investment Assets						
							All Investments	Publicly Traded Stocks	Other Marketable Securities	Mortgage Assets	Real Estate	Business Not Unit Managed	Miscellaneous Assets
$500,000 and Over	a	22	4	2	27	6	32	41	71	14	17	13	75
$200,000–499,999	1	13	4	3	17	7	22	24	12	28	12	40	8
$100,000–199,999	1	8	5	4	7	8	11	10	2	7	12	20	2
$50,000–99,999	4	14	11	10	18	17	15	14	6	23	22	6	5
$25,000–49,999	11	18	24	19	18	25	11	7	5	13	21	14	5
$10,000–24,999	23	18	36	30	9	23	7	3	4	12	13	6	3
$5,000–9,999	16	5	12	15	3	7	1	1	1	2	2	*	1
$1,000–4,999	19	2	4	13	*	5	*	*	*	2	1	*	*
$1–999	16	*	*	5	*	1	*	*	*	*	*	*	*
Zero	8	*	*	*	*	*	*	*	*	*	*	*	*
Negative b	2	*	*	–1	*	*	*	*	*	*	*	*	*
All Units b	100	100	100	100	100	100	100	100	100	100	100	100	100

Source: Dorothy S. Projector and Gertrude S. Weiss, *Survey of Financial Characteristics of Consumers* (Washington, D.C.: Board of Governors of the Federal Reserve System, August 1966), p. 136.

a Less than ¾ of 1 percent.

b Percents may not add up to 100 due to rounding.

Other notes: See Table 7, notes a–g.

Table 10 Wealth Concentration Patterns Within Types of Asset and Across Wealth Classes, 1962

Wealth Size	Asset Type (1)	(2)	(3)	(4)	(5)	(6)	(7)	(8)	(9)	(10)
$500,000 and Over			#		#	#	@	*	@	#
$100,000–499,999			#	*	#		#	#	#	@
$50,000–99,999	@	@	*	*	@		#	#		
$25,000–49,999	#	*	*	#			@	#	@	
$10,000–24,999	#	#		#			@	@		
$5,000–9,999	@	*								
$1,000–4,999		@								
$1–999										
Zero										
Negative										

Source: Dorothy S. Projector and Gertrude S. Weiss, *Survey of Financial Characteristics of Consumers* (Washington, D.C.: Board of Governors of the Federal Reserve System, August 1966), p. 136.

Key: @ refers to less than 15 percent but 10 percent or more of the total wealth of the asset.

  * refers to less than 20 percent but 15 percent or more of the total wealth of the asset.

  # refers to 20 percent or more of the total wealth of the asset.

Asset Types: (1) home equity; (2) auto equity; (3) equity in directly managed business or profession; (4) liquid assets; (5) publicly traded stocks; (6) other marketable securities; (7) mortgage assets; (8) real estate equity; (9) equity in a business not managed by the unit; (10) miscellaneous assets, mostly trust funds.

dominant in any asset type. Only with respect to equity in autos do we see any significant role played by these four intervals. This suggests that the four intervals represent a mass of consumer units virtually excluded from significant property-based power. These units clearly must find a basis for power in other areas. Collectively, they included 45 percent of all consumer units in 1962. We recall that the only asset types in which many of them hold equity are autos and liquid accounts, with some home equity at the upper interval. For analytical purposes, we regard them as a *propertyless underclass*. Indeed, they held as their share only 2 percent of total wealth.

Less obvious but reasonably clear is the essential contrast in form of wealth for those above and below the $50,000 line. Below this line are the broad middle ranks wherein wealth is held primarily in assets associated with family economics. These consumer units dominate the distribution of equity in homes and autos. Rather surprisingly, they also dominate the distribution of liquid assets, although they meet a fairly strong challenge from the wealthier consumer units. They are not dominant but hold substantial wealth shares in real estate, mortgage assets, and directly managed businesses or professions. Basically, they represent the successful ranks of those who serve but do not substantially own the central forms of capitalist wealth. In this sense, they may be called *pseudocapitalists*. While possessing some business, profession, and investment wealth, they held their wealth primarily in homes and liquid assets, and in those categories they were dominant. Comprising 50 percent of all consumer units, the pseudocapitalists held 41 percent of the total wealth of 1962.

Above the $50,000 line are the *estate capitalists*. We employ this term to convey two central features of their wealth situation. First, the magnitude of their average wealthholding places them in the class of units so rich as to be subject to federally imposed estate taxes. Second, their wealth is held in forms that are central to the definition and operation of the capitalist economy and, further, they possess overwhelming dominance in the distribution of ownership of those forms. Collectively, these units held 80 percent of all investment wealth, 69 percent of all wealth in directly managed businesses or professions, and 90 percent of all wealth in miscellaneous (trust) assets. Indeed, they held 57 percent of total wealth. Yet, together they comprise only about 6 percent of all consumer units.

Not only did the estate capitalists dominate the distribution of investments in the aggregate—they also dominated each and every one of the specific types of investment assets covered in the 1962 survey. Their dominance was especially evident with respect to publicly traded stock and other marketable securities; however, in no investment asset type nor in business holdings of either type did their dominance receive serious challenge. The basic three-class wealth pyramid found in the 1962 study can be summarized by the size distributions given in Table 11.

FURTHER EVIDENCE ON PATTERNS OF WEALTHHOLDING

It is unfortunate that beyond the 1962 Federal Reserve study there exist only scattered wealth data. Most later wealth data do not cover the full

Table 11 Percentage Shares of Wealth and Wealth in Specific Assets, Three Wealth Classes of the United States, 1962 Consumer Units

			Percentage Shares of Total:									
	Consumer	Total					Asset Type					
Wealth Class	Units	Wealth	(1)	(2)	(3)	(4)	(5)	(6)	(7)	(8)	(9)	(10)
Estate												
Capitalists $50,000 and Over	6	57	24	19	69	38	89	91	72	63	79	90
Pseudo-												
Capitalists $5,000–49,999	50	41	72	64	30	55	11	10	27	36	20	9
Propertyless												
Underclass $4,999 or below	45	2	4	17	1	6	[a]	[a]	2	1	1	1
All Units	100	100	100	100	100	100	100	100	100	100	100	100

Source: Dorothy S. Projector and Gertrude S. Weiss, *Survey of Financial Characteristics of Consumers* (Washington, D.C.: Board of Governors of the Federal Reserve System, August 1966), p. 136.

Asset Types: (1) home equity; (2) auto equity; (3) equity in directly managed business or profession; (4) liquid assets; (5) publicly traded stocks; (6) other marketable securities; (7) mortgage assets; (8) real estate equity; (9) equity in a business not managed by unit; (10) miscellaneous assets, mostly trusts.

[a]Less than ½ of 1 percent.

range of the wealth distribution. And those that do are not of adequate quality or quantity to allow confident comparison with the 1962 data for purposes of trend analyses. The best data beyond that already cited come from studies of the very rich and from estimates of their wealth based on the *estate-multiplier method* of extrapolating data from estate tax filings. Before discussing these data we pause to comment on an example of the limited full-range data that are available.

The general absence of good data on wealth distributions over time is curious when cast against the myth of egalitarianism in the United States and the massive data available on other aspects of the economy and the social order. In all probability the structure of wealth is not irrelevant to this absence. Be that as it may, it is also curious that the few data that can conceivably be compared directly to the 1962 data are again based on an interest in consumer characteristics. Perhaps only the pecuniary motive enables the system to tolerate the collection of such data.

Our thanks go to the University of Michigan's Survey Research Center for comparison data on the financial characteristics of consumers. For a number of years, SRC has published a series on consumer finances. Although size distributions of wealthholding are not standard in those publications, occasionally they do appear in secondary analyses. Bach and Stephenson[7] have prepared such a distribution from the 1969 SRC data. Unfortunately, they do not present their distribution by quintiles, nor do the wealth intervals of their distribution correspond exactly with those for the 1962 study.

Nevertheless, there is a rough correspondence between Bach and Stephenson's wealth intervals and those of the 1962 study. The major difficulty is the failure of these authors to break an interval at the $50,000 line that we found separated the estate capitalists from those below. Instead, the nearest break occurs at $60,000. In addition, these authors do not provide the narrower wealth bands at the top. Finally, there are reasons to suspect that the 1969 SRC data severely underestimates the asset holdings of the wealthy. Bach and Stephenson have compared estimates of aggregate wealth in asset types, as blown up for the general population from the SRC data, with estimates from the highly reliable Federal Reserve flow-of-funds data prepared for the Securities and Exchange Commission's study of institutional investors. They find that roughly 75 percent of all monetary assets (money and short-term debt, bonds, mortgages, and life insurance or pension reserves) were missed. At the same time, of the aggregate value of common stock and equity in unincorporated businesses, 45 percent was missed. As we have seen from the 1962 data, except for life insurance and pension fund reserves, the wealthiest consumer units dominate these asset types. Thus, we may anticipate that the 1969 SRC data understate the concentration of wealth at the top. In any case, Bach and Stephenson present the data of Table

12 on percentage shares of wealth by size of net worth of household in 1969.

If we cast the distribution of Table 12 in terms of our three classes of wealthholders, we must decide on an upper limit to the middle class. It makes sense to accept the cutoff at $60,000 and to keep in mind that this is $10,000 higher than in the prior data. If we do so, we find that the estate capitalists comprised 6 percent of the households and held 41 percent of the total wealth. The pseudocapitalists comprised 52 percent of households and held 52 percent of the total wealth. The underclass made up the remaining 41 percent of households but held only 7 percent of the total wealth.

Table 12 Percentage Shares of Total Assets ($1,622,000,000,000) by Size of Net Worth of Household, Early 1969

Net Worth	Percent of Households	Percent of All Assets
Negative	5	1
$0–1,999	24	2
$2,000–4,999	12	4
$5,000–9,999	14	7
$10,000–14,999	10	8
$15,000–24,999	14	13
$25,000–59,999	14	24
$60,000–99,999	3	10
$100,000 and Over	3	31
All Units	99	100

Source: G. L. Bach and James B. Stephenson, "Inflation and the Redistribution of Wealth," *The Review of Economics and Statistics* 56, 1(February 1974):1–13. Computed from Table 4, p. 6.

Compared to the 1962 data, the SRC data for 1969 suggest greater equality of wealthholding with the three analytic classes remaining about the same in their relative populations. The middle class comes out roughly as would be expected under distributional proportionality. The inequality of shares (not levels) stems from inbalance between the upper and lower tails of the distribution. All of this, however, is predicated on ignoring the underreporting of wealth at the estate level and the broader wealth band defining the middle class. We suggest that when these factors are taken into account, there is a remarkable similarity between the 1962 and 1969 aggregate wealth size distributions. Unfortunately, the reader must weigh these remarks carefully against the data deficiencies and other factors which might bias them. There is little credence to the belief that wealth inequality had radically decreased over the seven-year interval.

Prior to 1945, according to Lampman,[8] no more than ten scholars had attempted to construct size distributions of wealth for the United States. The break in this situation came with Horst Mendershausen's study, "The Pattern of Estate Tax Wealth,"[9] wherein the estate-multiplier method[10] was introduced to American economists. This method became the primary tool in Lampman's fundamental study[11] of the shares of wealth held by top wealthholders in the United States from 1922 to 1956. Subsequently, Smith[12] extended the application of the method to IRS data for selected years to 1969 and improved on the estimates of the earlier studies.

From the series of size distributions developed from estate tax returns, we have gained an appreciation of the general stability of the high wealth concentration over the first two-thirds of the twentieth century in the United States. While wealth has become less concentrated over family units and persons during this period, the decline has not been great and has been centered in years of exceptional economic duress or governmental management of the economy. The concentration of wealth increased during the 1920s, decreased during the Great Depression, World War II, and the early Cold War, increased once more during the Korean War and middle 1950s, and remained stable through 1969. Data for the years since 1969 are insufficient for further assessment of the trend.

The basic limitation of size distributions estimated by the estate-multiplier method is their coarseness at the lower end. This limitation does not seriously affect the ability of this method to demonstrate the high degree of wealth concentration. Those who are subject to estate taxation are already wealthy in comparison with the general population. Thus, showing that wealth is concentrated among that segment of the population having estate tax liability is tantamount to demonstrating the high concentration of wealth at the top. And, because even the estate-multiplier method appears to generate conservative estimates, the demonstration achieves an unusually high empirical validity.

Lampman's classical study of wealth shares showed that the concentration of wealth was highest on the eve of the Great Depression. In 1929, the richest 0.5 percent of Americans owned 32.4 percent of total net wealth of individuals. With the Depression, however, the fortunes of the rich plunged, and the rich became less rich. By 1933 the top 0.5 percent of Americans were holding 25.2 percent of net individual wealth, a sharp decline from its share of four years earlier. Interestingly, this apparent nadir coincided with the beginning of the New Deal. Indeed, much of the decline in the share of the top 0.5 percent from 1929 to 1933 had been restored by 1939 when FDR's emphasis on social programs hit its nadir. In any case, the wealth share of the top 0.5 percent stood at 28.0 percent by 1939.

During World War II, wealth concentration decreased, and by 1945 the top 0.5 percent of wealthholders held only 20.9 percent of total net individual wealth. This decline apparently had leveled out by 1949, the year for which available data show the lowest inequality of wealthholding. In that year the top 0.5 percent of wealthholders held 19.3 percent of privately held net wealth. Thereafter, inequality increased again, and by 1953 the top 0.5 percent had brought their share back to roughly

22.0 percent of total private net wealth. Practically no change in this share was found for the years 1958 and 1962, although by 1965 the share of the top 0.5 percent had risen to 23.7 percent.[13] Data for 1969 indicate that the top 0.5 percent held only 19.9 percent of total net wealth of persons. Whether these fluctuations in estimates after World War II reflect real changes or data unreliability cannot be said. In either case, their trend shows a stable, high degree of concentration of net wealth at the top. The richest 0.5 percent of the United States population has consistently held about 22.0 percent of personal wealth over the last thirty years. (The corresponding pattern for the top 1 percent of wealth-holders was given earlier in Table 3.)

Despite the high stability of concentrated wealth shares held by the richest Americans, some changes apparently have occurred in the postwar period. Most significant of these has been the diffusion of ownership of corporate stock. The share of this asset held by the very wealthiest individuals has declined. The decline has accompanied a fivefold increase in stocks traded on the New York Stock Exchange from 1952 to 1970. Lower-level estate capitalists and some higher-level pseudocapitalists have been the prime beneficiaries of this expansion. The aggregate decline of dominance in stock ownership by the top 0.5 percent and 1.0 percent of wealthholders is shown in Table 13. While the percentage share of corporate stock fell, between 1953 to 1969, from 86.3 percent to 50.8 percent for the richest 1 percent, it fell from 77.0 percent to 44.0 percent for the richest 0.5 percent of wealthholders.

As we have previously noted, the estate class of wealthholders is the true capitalist class, for the bulk of their holdings is in corporate stock, real estate, and other capital instruments. Further, their holdings form the dominant portion of these capital goods. Discussion of the evidence for these claims is obstructed by the problems of access to the data on wealth. Most of our data comes from governmental sources, which maintain tight control over it to protect the identity of top wealthholders. And so we must work with data that have been codified and disseminated for other purposes. The arbitrarily imposed cutoff lines between the wealth classes in the available data present a technical problem. These lines do not always correspond to the best analytic divisions, nor are they necessarily comparable between data sets.

When we invoked the rubric *estate capitalists* as a label for the richest wealthholders in the 1962 Federal Reserve study, we did so to emphasize the distinction between that class and the poorer classes of wealthhold-ers. Thus, we are saying that the wealth of estate capitalists is so great that it calls into question the myth of egalitarianism and justifies some public action.

Technically, we had to rely on cutoff points already built into the data. Thus, we chose the floor for our class of estate-capitalists so that the *mean* wealth was of estate size. Unfortunately, this meant that some

Table 13 Percentage Shares of Richest[a] 0.5 Percent and 1.0 Percent of Persons in National Wealth of United States, 1953, 1958, 1962, 1965, and 1969

	1953		1958		1962		1965		1969	
	Share Held by Richest 0.5% (percent)	1.0%	Share Held by Richest 0.5% (percent)	1.0%	Share Held by Richest 0.5% (percent)	1.0%	Share Held by Richest 0.5% (percent)	1.0%	Share Held by Richest 0.5% (percent)	1.0%
Real Estate[b]	10.3	15.5	10.1	15.1	10.3	15.3	10.3	14.8	9.8	14.4
Corporate Stock[c]	77.0	86.3	66.6	75.4	53.3	62.0	53.2	61.2	44.0	50.8
Bonds	45.3	52.6	36.0	41.4	35.1	40.6	55.5	61.0	32.0	35.9
Cash[d]	13.1	18.0	10.4	15.2	10.4	15.3	11.9	17.1	9.7	14.4
Debt Instruments[e]	24.1	32.1	28.6	37.3	32.0	42.3	37.1	47.7	30.2	34.7
Life Insurance (CSV)[f]	10.2	14.1	9.4	14.1	7.6	11.4	6.1	10.2	6.6	10.8
Miscellaneous and Trusts[g]	12.3	15.9	13.3	15.4	——	——	16.6	19.8	15.2	19.0
Trusts	85.4	91.7	85.1	92.1	——	——	85.2	91.7	85.8	91.6
Miscellaneous	5.6	8.9	6.3	7.9	10.5	13.9	8.0	10.8	7.4	10.8
Total Assets	21.2	26.7	20.4	25.5	20.7	26.2	22.1	27.4	19.3	24.4
Liabilities[h]	15.2	20.7	12.9	16.8	15.2	19.4	13.8	17.7	13.6	18.0
Net Worth	22.0	27.5	21.7	26.9	21.6	27.4	23.7	29.2	20.4	25.6
Number of Persons (in millions)	0.80	1.60	0.87	1.74	.93	1.87	.97	1.94	1.01	2.03

Source: James D. Smith and Stephen D. Franklin, 1974, "The Concentration of Personal Wealth, 1922-1969," *American Economic Review* 64, 2(May):162-167, from Table 1, p. 166.

[a]"Richness" is measured in terms of gross assets. Net worth is preferred to gross assets as a classifier, but the microdata that would have permitted such an arrangement have been destroyed by the IRS.

[b]Real estate is shown at its market value without deduction of mortgages, liens, or other incumbrances. Included in real estate are land and structures for personal and business use. All other business assets are included in the "Miscellaneous" category. Real estate held in trust is included here to the extent of the trust interest. A relatively small proportion of trust assets is in real estate, but the absolute value of all trust assets is understated here.

[c]Corporate stock includes the value of all common and preferred issues, shares in domestic or foreign firms whether traded or closely held, certificates and shares of building and loan and savings and loan associations, Federal Land Bank stock, and other instruments representing an equity interest in an enterprise. Accrued dividends are also included. Stock held in trust is included, but the absolute value is understated.

[d]Cash includes balances in checking and savings accounts, currency on hand or in safety deposit boxes, cash balances with stock brokers, and postal savings accounts. Cash in trust is included, but understated.

[e]Debt instruments include notes and mortgages, security credit, and similar assets owned by individuals.

[f]Life insurance (cash surrender value—CSV) is the amount individuals could expect to receive were they to surrender their policies to the carriers. It takes account of policy loans, accrued dividends and unearned premiums.

[g]"Miscellaneous and Trusts" includes all assets owned in trust *except real estate* and all assets other than real estate, corporate stock, bonds, cash, debt instruments, and life insurance (CSV) not held in trusts. Included are such items as consumer durables, personal effects, business assets (excluding real estate), mineral rights, tax sale certificates, judgments, lifetime transfers, and growing crops if not included in the value of real estate. This classification is shown here as an information item. It should not be summed with other assets to arrive at a total asset figure because trust assets are included within the individual asset types. Miscellaneous assets are those described under "Miscellaneous and Trusts" less trust assets. The miscellaneous asset category is added to other assets to arrive at total assets. Trusts represent the actuarial value of reversionary and remainder interests in trusts. This actuarial value is substantially less than the total market value of assets held in trusts. The separate value of trusts could be estimated directly only for 1965. For other years indirect estimates were made. The value for trusts is shown as an information item. The assets held in trust have been distributed to specific asset categories.

[h]Liabilities include all legal obligations except loans on life insurance policies.

of the persons in this class did not, strictly speaking, fall within the analytic class of estate-capitalists.

ESTATE CAPITALISTS: TOP WEALTHHOLDERS AND THE SUPERRICH

When we concentrate on the series of size distributions for wealthholding based on IRS estate tax returns, we find a similar technical problem. The earliest distributions employ the concept of *top wealthholders*, defined as those persons with *gross* assets of $60,000 or more as estimated from estate tax returns. This concept ignores the fact that a person with $70,000 gross assets and $30,000 debt would be included among top wealthholders while another person with $50,000 gross assets and $10,000 debt would not. Yet the two would have identical net wealth. The refusal of IRS to allow researchers to examine microfiles and individual returns prevents us from correcting for this problem. In recent years, pressures in Congress have resulted in more access, and the latest series of analyses employ the concept of the *superrich*, defined as those whose net wealth (gross assets less debts) is $60,000 or more. Thus, the superrich class of the latest series corresponds much more closely to our analytic class of estate-capitalists and provides a source of detailed information on the aggregate characteristics of this class. For the earlier data, however, we must fall back on the concept of *top wealthholders*. In most instances, conclusions from data on top wealthholders will differ very little from those based on data on the superrich. Both concepts produce wealth classes of estate-capitalists.

In Table 14, we see the significance of capitalist ownership in the wealth of top wealthholders during the 1950s and 1960s. This table shows that ownership of corporate stock has consistently been the primary

Table 14 Composition of Wealth Held by Top Wealthholders, 1953, 1958, 1962, and 1969

Item	1953	1958	1962	1969[a] Comparable Basis	New Basis
Total Assets (billions)	355.9	542.0	752.0	1,445.0	1,580.6
Percent in Corporate Stock	39.6	42.6	43.3	34.6	34.9
Percent in Real Estate	23.0	24.5	25.0	26.9	27.1
Percent in Other Assets[b]	12.4	12.1	9.8	16.0	14.9
Percent in Cash	9.5	8.5	9.4	11.7	12.0
Percent in Bonds	10.0	6.6	6.4	5.3	5.4
Percent in Notes and Mortgages	3.5	3.8	4.0	3.7	3.8
Percent in Insurance Equity	2.0	2.0	2.1	1.9	2.0
Debts (billions)	31.8	49.6	82.7	188.6	203.6
Net Worth (billions)	324.1	492.4	669.3	1,256.4	1,377.0

Source: Internal Revenue Service, "Statistics of Income—1969, Personal Wealth Estimated from Estate Tax Returns," Publication 482 (10-73) (Washington, D.C.: Government Printing Office, 1973), p. 59.

[a]Improved mortality rates information was used to calculate new estimates for 1969, although prior methods were used to calculate estimates on a basis comparable to prior years.

[b]Primary component, probably, in trusts or lifetime transfers: instruments for transmitting assets in anticipation of death and to avoid taxation or reduce tax rates.

component of rich estates. But real estate ownership has also played a major role. Corporate stock and real estate have continually comprised over 60 percent of the wealth of the top wealthholders. Along with cash and bonds, corporate stock and real estate have steadily formed 80 percent of top wealthholder wealth.

The number of top wealthholders has increased over the years and by 1969 totaled between 6.98 and 9.01 million individuals, depending on which set of estimates one accepts. The lower estimate is given by Smith,[14] who has provided the most recent account and most of the data on the superrich. The higher estimate is reported in the official IRS (1973) analysis of personal wealth from 1969 estate tax returns.[15] Thus, top wealthholders are estimated to have comprised from 5.6 percent to 7.4 percent of the 1969 midyear adult population in the United States in 1969.

The disparity between these estimates results from the estate-multiplier method of estimating wealthholding in the general population and from technical variations in the application of this method. The key assumption of the method is that death takes a probability sample of the population each year. Mortality rates describe death's sampling ratios. Thus, if we know mortality rates for persons by characteristics, we can estimate the distribution of such characteristics in the general population by utilizing recorded data on death's sample. On the average, death annually provides a one-percent sample, which can be statistically enlarged by inverse mortality rates to estimate the wealthholding distribution for the general population. Variation in mortality rates, sample characteristics attended to, and technical aspects of the enlargement can produce variations in the final estimates. Such variations of procedure explain, in part, the disparities between the estimates provided by the IRS and by Smith.

The superrich, described by Smith, are persons who hold net worth of at least $60,000. They form a subset of the top wealthholders or those who possess gross assets of $60,000. Top wealthholders form an elite subset of the general population. It is informative to compare these overlapping populations with respect to patterns and extent of wealthholding. For this purpose, we follow Smith's data on the superrich and the IRS count of top wealthholders.

National personal wealth, in 1969, was $3,514.8 billion and national personal net worth was $3,090.2 billion. According to the IRS, nine million persons, or 7.4 percent of the adult population of 1969, held individual gross wealth of at least $60,000. These top wealthholders held $1,580.6 billion gross wealth and $1,377.0 billion net worth or 45.0 percent and 44.6 percent, respectively, of the national totals. The average gross wealth of individuals in the general population was roughly $17,000. However, the average gross wealth for top wealthholders was $175,369. The average net worth of top wealthholders was $152,779. Quite obviously, wealth was very unequally distributed. Even among top wealthholders there were notable inequalities.

Top wealthholders may be differentiated by size of net worth, a measure of wealth that is generally to be preferred over gross wealth. Their holdings can also be differentiated by type of asset. Appendix Table A3 provides a tabulation of the wealth of top wealthholders in 1969 according to these two modes of differentiation. Table 15 gives the same tabulation in percentages that allow direct comparison of the asset composition of wealth at different levels of net worth.

Table 15 Composition of Wealth Held by Top Wealthholders, by Asset and Size of Net Worth, 1969

Item	All Top Wealth-holders (percent)	Size of Net Worth				
		Under $50,000 (percent)	$50,000 to under $100,000 (percent)	$100,000 to under $300,000 (percent)	$300,000 to under $1,000,000 (percent)	$1,000,000 or more (percent)
Net Worth	87.1	47.2	85.9	89.8	90.8	91.7
Debts	12.9	52.8	14.1	10.2	9.2	8.3
Total Assets	100.0	100.0	100.0	100.0	100.0	100.0
Corporate Stock	34.9	10.3	18.4	29.8	43.8	56.0
Real Estate	27.1	54.1	39.4	31.0	20.3	8.6
Cash	12.0	8.9	18.4	15.4	9.8	4.0
Bonds	5.4	0.1	3.6	4.2	6.4	9.3
Notes and Mortgages	3.8	2.3	3.9	4.7	4.4	1.9
Insurance Equity	2.0	8.3	2.9	1.8	1.0	0.4
Other Assets	14.9	15.2	13.4	13.1	14.3	19.9

Source: Computed from Table A3.

When we define top wealthholders by net worth classes, we see even more clearly the concentration of wealth in the hands of the very rich. Although by the standards of ordinary citizens all top wealthholders are exceedingly rich, within their own ranks some are richer than others. Given the IRS categories of net worth, the difference between net worth of $100,000 and net worth of $300,000 is significant among the rich.

Those with net worth of $300,000 or more comprised only 0.6 percent of the adult population and 8.5 percent of all top wealthholders. However, these extremely wealthy individuals held fully 42.3 percent of the assets of the rich and 19.0 percent of the total personal wealth of the nation.

Further, the net worth interval from $100,000 to $300,000 served as a transition category between rich persons whose wealth was centered in real estate and those whose wealth was centered in corporate stock ownership. The roles of real estate and corporate stock in the wealthholding of the just rich and the millionaire rich were in sharp contrast. Rich persons with net worth under $50,000 held 54.1 percent of their wealth in real estate and only 10.3 percent in corporate stock. But, the millionaire rich held only 8.6 percent of their wealth in real estate and fully 56.0 percent in corporate stock.

Not only are the very rich much richer than others, they also have greater freedom from debt. The millionaire rich held 91.7 percent of their wealth as net worth—that is, in assets unencumbered by debts. Top wealthholders in general held 87.1 percent of assets debt free. By contrast, recall that in 1962 8.1 percent of all families held no debt free assets and, indeed, held debts in excess of assets. Vast wealth and freedom from debt is probably the best economic insurance one can have. The very rich do not need great investments in insurance—at least not of the type known to the common citizen. And this is reflected in the small and declining role of insurance equity in their wealthholdings. The abundant security that comes with vast wealth is also reflected in the pattern of investments in bonds. Bond ownership is basically a wealth form exclusive to the richer of the rich. In part this is because they are so economically secure that they can afford the luxury of bond investment. Bonds are often sold only in denominations that restrict the market to the very rich, and the yield of bonds is often so low that they are attractive only to those who do not need high returns as much as they need to protect wealth already accumulated.

The significance of these patterns of wealthholding among the top wealthholders is correlated to the structure of wealth dominance. Table 16 summarizes the disproportionate wealthholding of top wealthholders. Here, too, we see the $100,000 to $300,000 net worth class as transitional. In this class, corporate ownership and possession of bonds are significant portions of the nation's total value in these assets. Top wealthholders held 70.6 percent and 72.3 percent, respectively, of the national total of corporate stock and monetary bonds. Those who possessed net worth of $100,000 or more comprised only 3.0 percent of the adult population but held 62.2 percent and 62.4 percent, respectively, of the national totals.

Table 16 Percentage Shares of Wealth, Net Worth, and Selected Assets, Top Wealthholders and Top Wealthholders by Size of Net Worth, 1969

Size of Net Worth, Top Wealthholders	Percent of Adults	Percent of Total Wealth	Percent of Total Net Worth	Selected Assets, Percent Held			
				Corporate Stock	Real Estate	Cash	Bonds
$1,000,000 or more	0.1	9.2	9.6	23.1	2.4	2.7	25.3
$300,000–1,000,000	0.5	9.8	10.2	19.4	5.9	7.1	18.7
$100,000–300,000	2.4	14.7	15.0	19.7	13.5	16.7	18.4
$50,000–100,000	2.9	8.6	8.4	7.1	10.0	11.6	9.2
Under $50,000	1.5	2.7	1.4	1.2	4.3	1.8	0.7
All Top Wealthholders	7.4	45.0	44.6	70.6	36.1	39.8	72.3
All Persons (adults)	100.0	100.0	100.0	100.0	100.0	100.0	100.0
Total Value (billions)	—	$3514.8	$3090.2	$781.3	$1187.0	$476.2	$118.0

Source: Computed from our Table 15 and information on United States totals supplied in James D. Smith, "The Concentration of Personal Wealth in America, 1969," *Review of Income and Wealth* 20, 2(June 1974):143–180.

CONCLUDING COMMENTS

It would be difficult to overestimate the significance of these findings. American values and beliefs have long supposed a consistency between capitalism and the general good. But if capitalism creates or maintains such disparities of wealth, how is this a general public good? The classical answer has been the "long run, trickle down" theory of economic progress. The claim is that those who accumulate private property are essential to economic progress because only vast accumulations can provide sufficient capital for ventures that create as well as exploit resources. Such ventures are supposed to add to the pool of resources available for distribution. Although the critical capital must necessarily reap the greater reward in this distribution, the incremental margin allows for a "trickle down" into the coffers of the general population. Over the long run, so the fable goes, this trickle will become a stream and everyone will rise to new heights of economic security if not outright equality. In the end, it is said, if not everyone is a capitalist, then at least everyone has equal opportunity.

Unfortunately, the classical answer fails to recognize that although systems may rightly be planned on teleological grounds, they ought not long be judged on those grounds. It accepts current suffering on a presumption of a different future. But today is yesterday's future. At some point even teleologically rationalized systems can be evaluated for their efficiency (or deficiency). When, after centuries of operation, a system remains so unequal that 3 percent of the adult population owns 35 percent of its net worth and over 60 percent of its institutionally critical wealth, it becomes imperative that we ask whether something is wrong.

In the history of human conflict there has always been a tendency for might to seek to be defined as right. Those who come, ultimately by use of force, to dominate others find it advantageous to seek ways of perpetuating that dominance without continued resort to force, with its costs or risks. The institution of government, or philosophically rationalized systems of control, is the prime example of this historical imperative. In practice, governments perform both political and juridical functions. Politically, they elaborate agencies and regulations for administering and overseeing the economic and organizational processes that benefit and maintain the dominance of the ruling class. Juridically, they codify and rationalize values and beliefs that support the class structure and adjudicate subsidiary disputes to remove threats to the system.

Thus, economic and political systems are never independent. Any discussion of income or wealth is implicitly a topic in *political* economy. This is easily seen when one examines the nature of capitalism. Capitalism implies a social system rationally constructed on the premise that wealth is the critical factor in economic production and, therefore, deserves disproportionate returns of power, income, and privilege. It is quintessentially a political economy of wealth. It is no accident that the theory of capitalism arose at a time when the ruling class was shifting from agrarian to industrial wealthholding. In the former system, ownership and wealth could be identified fairly easily with physical aspects of the productive economic processes. In the industrial system, wealth was obscured and could not be easily identified with observable contributions to the productive economic processes. New rationalizations for the disproportionate returns to wealth had to be constructed if the new ruling class was to solidify its dominance without great threats from below. To that end various economists, social philosophers, and others have been employed or have voluntarily stepped forth. Various legal devices have evolved to ensure that those with sufficient wealth can claim extraordinary security and exercise inordinate power.

Unequal distribution of wealth is of critical significance because wealth conditions the exercise of power and, through power, determines much of the inequality of social life. Among the consequences of wealth inequality is income inequality. Income refers to a *flow* of money or in-kind goods. Wealth refers to a *store* of the same. Income also refers to payment or *compensation for* something as part of an exchange. Wealth, however, refers essentially to *control over* something—not merely some thing, but something of central instrumental value. Although some would argue about whether income follows wealth or vice versa, it seems clear that control over things more often determines compensation than the reverse. That, of course, is not to deny the obvious fact that income begat by wealth adds to it.

In the capitalist state, the most critical form of wealth is that of ownership of organizational and legal instruments of economic production. Although ownership and control are not logically equivalent, capitalism makes them practically equivalent. And because those who are in control are in the best positions to determine the outcome of social processes, we expect them, as a class, to receive the greatest income from production. Corporate stocks, corporate and governmental bonds, real estate titles, notes and mortgages, trust funds, and savings accounts are all instruments for the production and control of economic resources and amenities. They arose in a context of power and privilege and, hence, serve to define it.

In the next chapter, we consider some of the ways the structure of wealth is related to inequality in income. We offer only illustrative material and do not intend the discussion as an exhaustive account. The intention is to show the inseparability of questions regarding income inequality and questions regarding wealth inequality. The processes by which the intimate connections between wealth and income are maintained are more thoroughly explored in Chapters 3 and 6.

NOTES

1. In the discussion of inequality in colonial and revolutionary America, we rely heavily on two sources: Sidney Lens' excellent history of poverty in America, *Poverty: America's*

Enduring Paradox (New York: Apollo Editions, 1971); and sections of Clarence H. Cramer's *American Enterprise: Free and Not so Free* (Boston: Little, Brown and Company, 1972).

2. Sidney Lens, *Poverty: America's Enduring Paradox* (New York: Apollo Editions, 1971), p. 81.

3. The information on Boston and Brooklyn given in Table 1 is discussed along with similar data in an especially interesting article by Edward Pessen, "The Egalitarian Myth and the American Social Reality: Wealth, Mobility, and Equality in the 'Era of the Common Man,' " *American Historical Review* 76, 4 (October 1973): 989–1034. Pessen details the difficulties and methods of calculating wealth differences from historical records. His paper gives much anecdotal information we have not utilized but which we recommend to the reader. For similar research that concentrates on the poverty-ridden masses of the nineteenth century, the reader is urged to consult Stephen Thernstrom's *Poverty and Progress* (New York: Atheneum Press, 1969).

4. Ideally such distributions ought to carry supplemental information about the aggregate size of population and wealth and the monetary values at the class limits. Many persons appear oblivious to the fact that, although it is often useful and necessary, standardization may obscure other pertinent information that we might like to recover.

5. Dorothy S. Projector and Gertrude S. Weiss, *Survey of Financial Characteristics of Consumers* (Washington, D.C.: Federal Reserve Board, 1966). Although the original report by Projector and Weiss fails to include negative and zero wealth classes in the vast majority of their tables, it is true that these authors provide a series of detailed tables analyzing the financial characteristics of consumers with incomes below the Social Security Administration's "low budget" income line. Still, the omission of these classes from the general table leaves the impression that everybody shares to some degree in the privately held wealth and gives a rosier glow to the data than they warrant.

6. We remind the reader that the mean wealth in any given class covers both those who hold some positive amount of wealth and those who hold none. Thus, for example, the $222,600 average value of wealth in trust funds for the top wealth class greatly understates the value of such holdings *for those who have trust fund wealth.* That follows from the finding that only 26 percent, still large relative to other wealth classes, held any beneficial interests in trusts.

7. G. L. Bach and James B. Stephenson, "Inflation and the Redistribution of Wealth," *The Review of Economics and Statistics* 56, 1 (February 1974): 1–13.

8. Robert J. Lampman, *Changes in the Share of Wealth Held by Top Wealth-Holders, 1922–1953* (New York: National Bureau of Economic Research, 1960), p. 2.

9. Horst Mendershausen, "The Pattern of Estate Tax Wealth," in Raymond W. Goldsmith, ed., *A Study of Savings in the United States*, Volume III (Princeton: Princeton University Press, 1956).

10. The reader interested in learning more about the technical aspects of the estate-multiplier method of estimating shares of wealthholding should consult such works as: Robert J. Lampman, *The Share of Top Wealth-Holders in National Wealth 1922–1956* (New York: National Bureau of Economic Research, 1962); James D. Smith and Staunton Calvert, "Estimating the Wealth of Top Wealth-Holders from Estate-Tax Returns," *Proceedings of the Business and Economics Section, American Statistical Association* (Washington, D.C.: Government Printing Office, 1965); James D. Smith, "The Concentration of Personal Wealth in America, 1969," *Review of Income and Wealth* 20, 2 (June 1974): 143–180.

11. Lampman, *The Share of Top Wealth-Holders.*

12. James D. Smith, "The Concentration of Personal Wealth in America, 1969," 143–180.

13. James D. Smith and Stephen D. Franklin, "The Concentration of Personal Wealth, 1922–1969," *American Economic Review* 64, 2 (May 1974): 162–167.

14. Smith, "The Concentration of Personal Wealth in America, 1969."

15. Internal Revenue Service, "Statistics of Income—1969, Personal Wealth Estimated from Estate Tax Returns," Publication 482 (10-73) (Washington, D.C.: Government Printing Office, 1973).

APPENDIX

Table A1 Average Dollar Value of Equity in Specific Assets Held by Consumer Units, by Wealth Size, December 31, 1962

Wealth Size[a]	Total Wealth	Own[b] Home	Auto-mobile	Business, Profession (farm and nonfarm)[c]	Liquid Assets[d]	Investment Assets[e]	Miscel-laneous Assets[f]
All Units:[g]	$ 20,982	$ 5,653	$ 644	$ 3,881	$ 2,675	$ 7,013	$ 1,116
$1–999	396	40	190	9	134	14	9
$1,000–4,999	2,721	1,298	445	83	701	170	25
$5,000–9,999	7,267	4,260	614	625	1,227	440	100
$10,000–24,999	16,047	8,852	850	1,499	2,624	2,054	168
$25,000–49,999	35,191	12,991	1,134	6,644	6,371	7,518	533
$50,000–99,999	68,980	14,167	1,499	16,719	10,858	24,556	1,181
$100,000–199,999	132,790	22,790	2,232	22,938	18,808	64,127	1,894
$200,000–499,999	300,355	25,889	2,326	72,516	21,007	169,052	9,564
$500,000 and over	1,260,667	56,232	2,679	295,035	46,094	628,271	232,355

Source: Dorothy S. Projector and Gertrude S. Weiss, *Survey of Financial Characteristics of Consumers* (Washington, D.C.: Board of Governors of the Federal Reserve System, August 1966), p. 110.

[a]Wealth: equity in named assets.

[b]Own home: principal residence and vacation homes.

[c]Business and profession: equities in family owned and operated businesses, professional practices, and farms.

[d]Liquid assets: checking accounts, savings, and United States savings bonds.

[e]Investment assets: marketable securities, investment real estate, and mortgages.

[f]Miscellaneous assets: largely assets held in personal trusts.

[g]Consumer unit: families and unrelated individuals as defined by the Bureau of the Census.

Table A2 Percentage of Consumer Units and Mean Wealth Held, Beneficial Interest in Trusts, by Wealth Class, 1962

Wealth Class	Percent of Units Holding Beneficial Interests	Mean Value (in dollars) of Beneficial Interests Held by Wealth Class
$1–999	[a]	[a]
$1,000–4,999	1	5
$5,000–9,999	1	62
$10,000–24,999	2	82
$25,000–49,999	2	159
$50,000–99,999	3	707
$100,000–199,999	2	655
$200,000–499,999	4	5,393
$500,000 and Over	26	222,600
All Units	1	937

Source: Dorothy S. Projector and Gertrude S. Weiss, *Survey of Financial Characteristics of Consumers* (Washington, D.C.: Federal Reserve Technical Paper, August 1966), Table A9, p. 113.

[a]Less than one-half of one percent, or less than one-half of one dollar.

Table A3 Number of Top Wealthholders and Asset Composition, by Size of Net Worth, 1969

Item	Total	Size of Net Worth				
		Under $50,000	$50,000 to under $100,000	$100,000 to under $300,000	$300,000 to under $1,000,000	$1,000,000 or more
Number of top Wealthholders (thousands)	9,013	1,815	3,497	2,937	642	121
		(billions of dollars)				
Total Assets	1,580.6	94.5	301.8	516.0	345.3	323.0
Real Estate	428.3	51.1	118.9	160.1	70.0	27.9
Corporate Stock	551.4	9.7	55.7	153.8	151.4	180.8
Bonds	85.3	0.8	10.9	21.7	22.1	29.9
Cash	189.7	8.4	55.4	79.3	33.7	12.9
Notes and Mortgages	59.4	2.2	11.8	24.2	15.1	6.0
Insurance Equity	31.0	7.8	8.7	9.4	3.6	1.3
Other Assets	235.8	14.4	40.3	67.4	49.5	64.2
Debts	203.7	49.9	42.7	52.4	31.6	26.9
Net Worth	1,377.0	44.6	259.1	463.6	313.7	296.1

Source: Internal Revenue Service, "Statistics of Income—1969, Personal Wealth Estimated from Estate Tax Returns," Publication 482 (10-73) (Washington, D.C.: Government Printing Office, 1973), Table A at p. 2.

Note: Detail may not add to totals due to rounding.

3
INCOME
DISTRIBUTION

Wealth and income inequality are closely connected. Wealth is created by the cumulative impact of income inequalities. The possession of wealth determines the capacity to generate income. Thus, wealth and income inequality must be examined together if an adequate picture of inequality in a society is to be developed.

In this chapter, we seek to understand the patterns of income inequality in America. Our efforts are thwarted, however, by the fact that the available data at many critical points are incomplete and dated. Access to Internal Revenue files is limited, and the government does not collect adequate survey data. Thus, it is impossible to determine accurately the complete profile of income distribution in America. Although *total* income distribution data are available up to the present, studies on the *types* and *forms* of income for various economic groupings are not as easily discovered—an interesting political fact in itself. Thus, our presentation is necessarily incomplete, but the existing data offer some general clues about the profile and pattern of income inequality.

THE OVERALL PROFILE OF INCOME INEQUALITY

How has the total income been distributed in America? Unfortunately, a definitive answer to this simple question is not available, primarily because the Census Bureau has systematically collected data on income only since 1947. There have been several attempts to estimate the pattern of total income for the years prior to 1947. One such attempt was made by Gabriel Kolko[1] who, unfortunately, had poor data with which to make his calculations. Nevertheless his findings, summarized in Table

1, provide a crude indicator of income inequality for various income fifths[2] between the years 1910 and 1947.

In Table 1, income fifths are determined in the same manner as in the tables in Chapter 2. The total income earning population is rank ordered by income, and equal groupings comprising successive 20 percents of the income earning population constitute each income fifth. The percentage of the total income—from all sources—is then reported for each fifth in selected years. The top and bottom income earning tenths are also reported, so that it is possible to visualize the shares of total income received by the top and the bottom of the income earning population.

Table 1 Percentage of Total National Income, Before Taxes, Received by Each Income Fifth[a]

Year	Lowest Fifth	Fourth Fifth	Middle Fifth	Second Fifth	Highest Fifth	Top 10 Percent	Bottom 10 Percent
1947	4.3	10.2	15.6	20.6	48.3	33.5	1.2
1946	4.0	11.0	16.0	22.0	47.0	32.0	1.0
1945	4.0	11.0	16.0	24.0	45.0	29.0	1.0
1941	3.0	9.0	16.0	22.0	50.0	34.0	1.0
1937	3.6	10.4	15.7	21.8	48.5	34.4	1.0
1934	5.9	11.5	15.5	20.4	46.7	33.6	2.1
1929	5.4	10.1	14.4	18.8	51.3	39.0	1.8
1921	5.2	10.5	13.9	19.4	51.0	38.2	2.0
1918	6.8	12.6	14.9	18.3	47.4	34.5	2.4
1910	8.3	11.5	15.0	19.0	46.2	33.9	3.4

Source: Gabriel Kolko, *Wealth and Power in America* (New York: Praeger, 1962), p. 14. © 1962 by Praeger Publishers. Reprinted by permission of Praeger Publishers and Thames & Hudson.

[a]Recalculated from percentages for tenths of population. Units are "recipients" for 1910–1937 and "spending units" for 1941–1947. Data sources were National Industrial Conference Board for 1910–1937 and the Survey Research Center for 1941–1947.

The figures in Table 1 reveal that the share of total income received by the bottom 20 percent of the population declined by almost one-half, while that of the highest income fifth remained about the same, hovering at around 47 percent of all income. Middle-income groupings received about the same shares of total income. These data, which must be interpreted cautiously, reveal enormous income inequality in America during the early years of this century. The upper 20 percent of the income-earning population received close to one-half of all income, with the other 80 percent receiving the other half. The top 10 percent received about one-third of the income in a given year. This indicates the capacity of the few to earn a proportion of all income about equal to that of the bottom three income fifths, or the bottom 60 percent of the income earning population.

What about more recent years? Has this pattern of income inequality changed? In Table 2, we present data on income distribution from the year 1929 up to the most recent available year, 1972. These data come from a variety of sources and can be considered comparable only for the years 1947 to 1972. Also, they overlap, for the years 1929 to 1974, with those presented by Kolko. Although there are small differences in the income figures for various income fifths, the overall pattern looks much the same for the two data sources.

As Table 2 indicates, the income share of the bottom fifth has stabilized at about 5 percent to 5.5 percent, while that of the top fifth has declined and stabilized at around 40 percent to 41 percent of all income earned

Table 2 Percentage Share of Money Income, Before Taxes, Received by Each Income-Fifth

Year	Lowest Fifth	Fourth Fifth	Middle Fifth	Second Fifth	Highest Fifth	Top 5 Percent
1973	5.5	11.9	17.5	24.0	41.1	15.5
1972	5.4	11.9	17.5	23.9	41.4	15.9
1971	5.5	11.9	17.4	23.7	41.6	15.7
1970	5.5	12.0	17.4	23.5	41.6	14.4
1969	5.6	12.3	17.6	23.5	41.0	14.0
1968	5.7	12.4	17.7	23.7	40.6	14.0
1967	5.4	12.2	17.5	23.7	41.2	15.3
1966	5.5	12.4	17.7	23.7	40.7	14.8
1965	5.3	12.1	17.7	23.7	41.3	15.8
1964	5.2	12.0	17.7	24.0	41.1	15.7
1963	5.1	12.0	17.6	23.9	41.4	16.0
1962	5.1	12.0	17.5	23.7	41.7	16.3
1961	4.8	11.7	17.4	23.6	42.6	17.1
1960	4.9	12.0	17.6	23.6	42.0	16.8
1959	5.0	12.1	17.7	23.7	41.4	16.3
1958	4.7	11.0	16.3	22.5	45.5	20.0
1957	4.7	11.1	16.3	22.4	45.5	20.2
1956	4.8	11.3	16.3	22.3	45.3	20.2
1955	4.8	11.3	16.4	22.3	45.2	20.3
1954	4.8	11.1	16.4	22.5	45.2	20.3
1953	4.9	11.3	16.6	22.5	44.7	19.9
1952	4.9	11.4	16.6	22.4	44.7	20.5
1951	5.0	11.3	16.5	22.3	44.9	20.7
1950	4.5	12.0	17.4	23.5	42.6	17.0
1949	3.2	10.5	17.1	24.2	45.0	18.3
1948	3.4	10.7	17.1	23.9	44.9	18.7
1947	5.0	11.8	17.0	23.1	43.0	17.2
1946	5.0	11.1	16.0	21.8	46.1	21.3
1945	3.8	11.0	17.2	24.0	44.0	17.6
1944	4.9	10.9	16.2	22.2	45.8	20.7
1941	4.1	9.5	15.3	22.3	48.8	24.0
1935–36	4.1	9.2	14.1	20.9	51.7	26.5
1929	(12.5)		13.8	19.3	54.4	30.0

Sources: U.S. Bureau of the Census, *Current Population Reports,* Series P-60, No. 85, Table 14 for the years 1947, 1950, and 1959–1971 (Washington, D.C.: Government Printing Office, 1972). Edward C. Budd, "Postwar Changes in the Size Distribution of Income in the U.S.," *American Economic Review* 60, 2(May 1970):247–260, Table 6, p. 255 for the years 1945, 1948, and 1949. U.S. Bureau of the Census, *Income Distribution in the United States* (a 1960 Census Monograph), by Herman P. Miller, p. 21 for the years 1929, 1935–1936, 1941, 1944, 1946, and 1951–1958 (Washington, D.C.: Government Printing Office, 1966). Data from the latter source were gathered by the Office of Business Economics.

in a given year. And the middle fifth shares have remained remarkably stable for at least twenty years. The shares of the top 5 percent have declined over the years, apparently fluctuating at around 14 percent to 16 percent of all income. Thus, although there has been some shift in the pattern of income distribution away from the top 20 percent, as well as from the top 5 percent, enormous differences in income distribution remain. The top 5 percent still receives about the same as the bottom 40 percent and the top 20 percent receives more than the bottom 60 percent.[3]

In analyses of the distribution of income by various fifths of the population, little is said about *how much* income is earned by individuals falling in various income fifths. How much, for example, is the average income of someone in the bottom, middle, or top fifth in a given year? In Table 3, we report the average income for families falling within various income fifths for the years 1947 to 1971—the last year for which data are readily available. The increasing amounts of income for all income fifths reflect the general increase in the standard of living of

Table 3 Mean Family Income Received by Each Fifth of Families: 1947–1971
Families Ranked by Size of Income (1971 constant dollars)

Year	All Families	Lowest Fifth	Second Fifth	Middle Fifth	Fourth Fifth	Highest Fifth	Top 5 Percent
1947	6,460	1,616	3,812	5,491	7,462	13,955	22,611
1948	6,212	1,522	3,727	5,374	7,205	13,232	21,246
1949	6,087	1,370	3,621	5,265	7,151	13,025	20,572
1950	6,451	1,451	3,838	5,613	7,547	13,805	22,322
1951	6,576	1,612	4,076	5,786	7,694	13,677	22,094
1952	6,869	1,682	4,189	5,942	8,002	14,527	24,315
1953	7,177	1,686	4,450	6,424	8,577	14,750	22,680
1954	7,099	1,598	4,259	6,283	8,483	14,873	23,286
1955	7,579	1,818	4,623	6,708	8,982	15,766	25,467
1956	8,022	2,006	4,973	7,140	9,507	16,526	26,313
1957	7,889	1,973	4,970	7,140	9,388	16,014	24,929
1958	7,950	2,027	4,929	7,115	9,420	16,256	25,120
1959	8,474	2,118	5,126	7,499	10,042	17,540	27,624
1960	8,761	2,146	5,256	7,710	10,338	18,397	29,435
1961	8,951	2,149	5,237	7,788	10,563	19,022	30,613
1962	9,118	2,325	5,471	7,979	10,805	19,011	29,724
1963	9,401	2,397	5,640	8,272	11,234	19,459	30,082
1964	9,709	2,525	5,825	8,593	11,650	19,952	30,680
1965	10,110	2,679	6,117	8,897	11,981	20,878	31,949
1966	11,029	3,199	7,004	9,760	12,904	22,333	33,307
1967	11,119	3,002	6,783	9,674	13,010	23,127	34,246
1968	11,399	3,249	7,068	10,088	13,452	23,198	32,146
1969	11,856	3,319	7,292	10,433	13,931	24,306	33,198
1970	11,800	3,245	7,080	10,266	13,864	24,543	33,983
1971	11,807	3,247	7,025	10,272	13,991	24,559	38,255

Source: Executive Office of the President: Office of Management and Budget, *Social Indicators, 1973* (Washington, D.C.: Government Printing Office, 1973), p. 179.

all Americans, as well as the impact of inflation. It should be emphasized that these are *average* figures—some earn more and some earn less than this average. Averaging of income is especially important in analyzing the income of the upper 20 percent or 5 percent, because this average conceals the truly enormous incomes of many superrich Americans.

INCOME AND WEALTH

One of the critical questions in analyzing income figures such as those in Tables 1, 2, and 3 is: How is income related to net wealth? We would expect that the wealthier an individual or family, the greater their income. High income creates wealth, and people with wealth possess the means to increase their wealth through activities that raise income. In Figure 1, the standard procedure for determining the degree of income and wealth inequality is represented. This procedure is known as the Lorenz curve. The curve is constructed in the following way. (1) What if there was perfect equality for income and wealth? Then each 10 percent of the people would receive 10 percent of the total income and hold 10 percent of the total wealth. In Figure 1, this hypothetical state is represented by the solid straight line which bisects the graph. As the solid line reveals, each increment in wealth or income corresponds to the same increment or percentage increase in families. Thus, 1 percent of wealth and income is held or earned by 1 percent of the families, 10 percent of the income or wealth by 10 percent of the families, 20 percent by 20 percent of the families, 40 percent by 40 percent of the families, and so on. (2) However, income and wealth are not distributed equally among families. This is reflected by the income and wealth curves in Figure 1. The further the curve—whether the income or wealth curve —from the perfect equality diagonal, the greater the inequality in income or wealth. Thus, from the relation of the curves to the diagonal, it is evident that there is considerably more wealth inequality than income inequality.[4] However, the distance between the two curves is only a gross indicator of how much more wealth inequality than income inequality there is; the curves should be interpreted separately in relation to the straight diagonal. (3) By drawing perpendicular lines from the curve to each axis of the graph, an indicator of what percentage of families hold what percentage of the total wealth or what percentage of the total income for the years 1970 and 1969, respectively, can be determined. This is done for the top 10 percent of wealthholders in 1970 and for wage earners in 1969.

Although the Lorenz curve is useful in depicting income and wealth inequality, it does not indicate the joint distribution of income and wealth. It reveals how much inequality there is for either wealth or income, but it does not indicate how they are correlated. That is, how much income are different levels of wealth likely to generate? Answers to this question will reveal the true relation between wealth and income inequality. Curiously, few data are available to provide an answer. Only one

Figure 1 Relation Between Income and Wealth

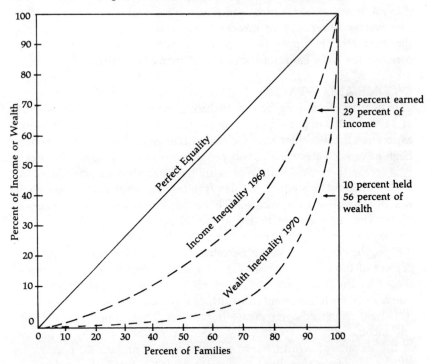

Source: Reprinted from the August 5, 1972 issue of *Business Week* by special permission. © 1972 by McGraw-Hill, Inc.

comprehensive study appears to have addressed this issue—the never-duplicated Federal Reserve Study of 1962.[5] From this one study, which is now more than a decade old, the joint distribution of income and wealth is reported.

In Table 4, we have reproduced this joint distribution. In this table the percentages of families of different levels of wealth (reported across the top of the table) earning different amounts of income (reported down the left side of the table) are summarized. The data are clear that the greater the wealth, the larger the income in 1962. For example, only 1 percent of those families with negative wealth (debts in excess of assets) earned between $10,000 and $15,000 in 1962, whereas 34 percent of those with net wealth between $10,000 and $25,000 earned this much. And, 35 percent of those worth $1,000,000 earned over $100,000 in 1962.

Perhaps this table seems like a long-winded way to say that wealth begets more income, and hence more wealth. But Table 4 reveals the *pattern* of this relationship between income and wealth. Just whether this pattern has remained stable or shifted in the last decade is, of course, impossible to determine. And it is an interesting political fact that only one glimpse at the relationship has been accorded those seeking to

Table 4 Joint Distribution of Income and Wealth of Families, 1962

Income (thousands)	All Families (percent)	Net Worth (thousands of dollars)										
		Negative	0–1	1–5	5–10	10–25	25–50	50–100	100–200	200–500	500–1,000	1,000 and up
0–3	100	12	31	16	15	17	7	1				
3–5	100	15	22	22	12	17	8	3				
5–7.5	100	7	14	21	17	28	8	4	1			
7.5–10	100	3	5	19	16	37	14	5	2			
10–15	100	1	3	9	13	34	24	11	4	1		
15–25	100		2	8	18	30	26	7	7	1		
25–50	100			1	2	7	20	31	30	5	3	
50–100	100				1	3	13	37	27	20		
100 and up	100						1	4		61	35	

Source: "Survey of Financial Characteristics," *Federal Reserve Bulletin* (March 1964), p. 291, as reported in Lester C. Thurow and Robert E. B. Lucas, "The American Distribution of Income: A Structural Problem," a study prepared for the use of the Joint Economic Committee, 92nd U.S. Congress (Washington, D.C.: Government Printing Office, 1972).

understand inequality in America. Why won't government collect the data? Answer: Because those with privilege and power don't want it collected—lest their privilege be exposed to the general population.

The next logical question thus becomes: In what ways, and in what quantities, does wealth generate income? It is one thing to visualize an overall pattern, or relationship, between wealth and income, but another to understand just how and why this pattern or relationship exists. As simple as this question may appear, its answer is difficult to provide, again primarily because the data are incomplete and somewhat dated.

In Table 5, we report the shares of the total income derived by various forms of activity: income from employee compensation, income from noncorporate entrepreneurial activity, and income from property. Employee compensation refers primarily to salaries and wages earned by workers, entrepreneurial income denotes small business and professional incomes from individual and family enterprises, and property income pertains to money earned through holding property, such as real estate, stocks, bonds, and the like.

Table 5 Property, Entrepreneurial, and Employee Shares in United States National Income (decade average percentages), 1900–1963

Years	Employee Compensation	(Noncorporate) Entrepreneurial	Property Income	Property Share by Source		
				Corporate Profit	Interest	Rent
1900–1909	55.0	23.7	21.3	6.8	5.5	9.0
1910–1919	53.6	23.8	22.6	9.1	5.4	8.1
1920–1929	60.8	17.5	21.7	7.8	6.2	7.7
1930–1939	67.5	14.8	17.7	4.0	8.7	5.0
1939–1948	64.6	17.2	18.2	11.9	3.1	3.3
1949–1958	67.3	13.8	18.9	12.5	2.9	3.4
1954–1963	69.9	11.9	18.2	11.2	4.0	3.0

Source: "Income Distribution: Functional Share," by Irving B. Kravis. Reprinted with permission of the publisher from *International Encyclopedia of the Social Sciences*, Volume 7, Edited by David L. Sills. Copyright © 1968 by Crowell Collier and Macmillan, Inc.

The data in Table 5 show that: (1) wages and other forms of employee compensation have increased as a proportion of total income since the turn of the century, (2) entrepreneurial income has fallen dramatically, and (3) property income has fallen, with corporate profits increasing, interest income falling slightly, and rent income falling dramatically.[6]

Although the proportions of total income derived from wage and salary, entrepreneurship, and property offer a general picture of the relative importance of different types of income, they do not reveal *which* income groups are likely to receive *what types* of income. In Table 6, wage, entrepreneurial, and property income, as well as pension or annuity income and other income sources, are presented for income fifths in 1962. Curiously, this is the most recently published data on types of income going to various income fifths.[7] This is the same "interesting political fact" previously cited. It is now 1975, soon 1976, 13 to 14 years after the prior study. The prior study is one of the most cited economic surveys in history—proof of its value. Yet, any one-shot survey is limited. Why no follow up? Why only this one study in the first place? We think because the feared uses of knowledge about wealth exceeds the desire of business for knowledge about consumers.

Table 6 Percentage Distribution of Income by Type and Income Fifth
of Recipients, 1962

Type of Income	Income Fifth					Top
	Lowest	Fourth	Middle	Second	Highest	5 Percent
Wages and Salaries	1	8	18	28	45	15
Business (entrepreneurial)	0	7	13	17	62	42
Property	4	8	10	11	65	47
Pensions and Annuities	30	33	13	11	12	6
Other	20	37	13	16	14	1
All Income	4	10	16	24	46	20

Source: Dorothy S. Projector, Gertrude S. Weiss, and Erling T. Thoresen, "Composition of Income as Shown by the Survey of Financial Characteristics of Consumers," in *Six Papers on the Size Distribution of Wealth and Income,* Lee Soltow, ed. (New York: National Bureau of Economic Research and Columbia University Press, 1969), Table 4, pp. 107–156.

As can be seen from Table 6, income from wages and salaries, businesses, and property is especially concentrated at the higher income levels. The top income fifth received 45 percent of all wages and salaries, 62 percent of all business income, and 65 percent of all property income in 1962. The top 5 percent of income recipients obtained 15 percent of wages and salaries, 42 percent of business income, and 47 percent of property income. Pensions and annuities, largely dominated by social security payments, and other income, including welfare payments, were more concentrated at lower income levels. The fact that different types of income are concentrated at different levels of the gross income distribution suggests a link between sources of income and income class. Most Americans rely upon wages as the primary source of income.[8] But, for many, wage or salary must be supplemented by (or substituted for) pensions, annuities, or welfare. The generally meager benefits of these added sources are concentrated at the bottom of the income distribution; hence, their receipt becomes a sign of relative deprivation. By contrast, at the top levels of income, wages and salaries are not so much supplemented as they are transcended. Although top income recipients may bring in high salaries, what distinguishes them as a group is their additional income from businesses and property, which (as we will analyze in Chapter 6) receives more favorable tax treatment than the income sources of the middle and lower groups.

Unfortunately, there are no data available on how different types of entrepreneurial income are distributed among various income fifths. There are, however, some rather old data on how types of property income are distributed among the five income fifths. These data are presented in Table 7. We already know from Table 6 that 65 percent of all property income goes to the top income fifth, with 47 percent going to the upper 5 percent. But the pattern of property income shows considerable variability, with income from stocks, trusts, and estates concentrated much more among top incomes than are interest, rents, and royalties. And as Table 7 underscores, virtually all dividends from closely-held, usually family-controlled, companies go to the top 5 percent. The reliance of the wealthy on stock dividends, trusts, and estates is predictable, because these forms of investment and wealthholding receive highly favorable tax treatment. Interest and rents also offer some tax benefits, but not to the degree afforded these other forms of property income.

Table 7 Distribution of Property Income by Income Fifths, 1962 (percent)

Type of Property Income	Income Fifth					Top 5 Percent
	Lowest	Fourth	Middle	Second	Highest	
All Property Income	4	8	10	11	65	47
Dividends from Publicly Traded Stock	2	4	9	4	82	64
Interest	9	12	11	18	51	30
Rents and Royalties	6	12	12	13	55	37
Trusts and Estates	2	2	1	7	88	64
Dividends from Closely Held Corporations[a]	0	0	0	0	100	93

Source: Dorothy S. Projector, Gertrude S. Weiss, and Erling T. Thoresen, "Composition of Income as Shown by the Survey of Financial Characteristics of Consumers," in *Six Papers on the Size Distribution of Wealth and Income,* ed. Lee Soltow (New York: National Bureau of Economic Research and Columbia University Press, 1969), Table 11, pp. 107–156.

[a]Corporations primarily owned by unit but not directly managed by unit.

INCOME INEQUALITY: AN OVERVIEW

The data, as imperfect and dated as they are, clearly expose a pattern of vast income inequality in America. This pattern seems to be the result of wealth holdings that provide the upper-income groups with sources of income not available to most wage-earning Americans. In Chapter 1 we presented several elementary principles of inequality. In Chapters 2 and 3 we have summarized the data on the extent, degree, and pattern of inequality in American society.

It is necessary now to elaborate these elementary principles into a more adequate model for explaining why and how such vast inequality—whether measured in terms of wealth or income—exists in America. And so, the remaining chapters of this book are devoted to developing a sociological explanation of the data on inequality.

NOTES

1. Gabriel Kolko, *Wealth and Power in America* (New York: Frederick A. Praeger, Inc., 1962).

2. Kolko's data were presented as income tenths, but we have converted them to income fifths to keep them comparable to the presentation in Chapter 2 and accepted reporting procedures.

3. After-tax distributions of income show little change from before-tax distributions. This is most thoroughly shown by Benjamin A. Okner, "Individual Taxes and the Distribution of Income," chapter 3 in James D. Smith, ed., *The Personal Distribution of Income and Wealth* (New York: National Bureau of Economic Research, 1975), pp. 45–73. Ignoring wealthfare other than through taxes and looking at individual taxes and welfare transfers, Okner finds that of the small reduction in inequality produced by these, 75 percent comes from welfare. Only 25 percent of this small combined reduction can be attributed to tax redistribution.

4. The divergence of the Lorenz curve from the diagonal of perfect equality can be summarized in a quantitative index of inequality known as the Gini index or coefficient of concentration. This coefficient is equal to twice the area between the Lorenz curve of actual distribution and the line of equal distribution. The nearer the coefficient to 1.0, the greater the inequality. For example, Technical Paper 17 of the U.S. Bureau of the Census reports Gini coefficients for family income as varying between .351 and .379 during the years 1947–1964. Gini coefficients for individuals during the same period are reported as varying between .476 and .568. Unfortunately, few studies report Gini coefficients by type of income. Exceptions are Kravis' *The Structure of Income* (Philadelphia: University of Pennsylvania), for 1950, and Projector, Weiss, and Thoresen, "Composition of Income as Shown by the Survey of Financial Characteristics of Consumers," in Lee Soltow, ed., *Six Papers on the Size Distribution of Wealth and Income* (New York: National Bureau of Economic Research, 1969), for 1962. Kravis reports Gini coefficients of .35, .60, and .38 for "wages and salaries," "property income," and "total income," respectively. Projector and colleagues report Gini coefficients of .52, .93, and .43 for "wages and salaries," "business and property income," and "total income," respectively. The differences between these estimates raise numerous questions of both substance and method. The estimates, however, are consistent in showing greater inequality among families for property income than for wages and salaries. The relative contribution of inequality of a given type to total income inequality depends, of course, upon the functional distribution of income, that is, the relative importance of types. Pryor is one of the few persons who have attempted to assess the contribution of property inequality to the total Gini. His estimate is that, when other inequality is taken as given, property inequality raises the Gini for United

States families by as much as .06, a fairly substantial increment that still ignores indirect effects. See Frederick L. Pryor, *Property and Industrial Organization in Communist and Capitalist Nations* (Bloomington: Indiana University Press, 1973).

5. Although it is true that the annual Survey of Consumer Finances, conducted by the Survey Research Center at the University of Michigan's Institute for Social Research, has occasionally reported both income and asset distributions for its respondents, we have been unable to find any analysis of joint distribution. In any case, there are severe limitations to the SRC data for these purposes—not the least of which is the problem of sample adequacy at the upper reaches of income and wealth. Nevertheless, the student of income dynamics would be well advised to study the SCF data for trends in income distribution. In addition, ongoing SRC studies have now produced a five-year panel study of five thousand American families and their incomes. Preliminary reports are currently available. The basic findings so far reported are that attitudes and economic behavior are of little consequence for income change; the only magic in economic success is in where one starts from and factors of family composition related to earning power or economic dependency. Unfortunately, little attention has yet been given to the relation of wealth to income.

6. A problem with the presentation in Table 5 is that it fails to appreciate the affinity between property income and private entrepreneurial activity. Some income included in "noncorporate entrepreneurial" refers to self-employment wage or salary. Other income in this category, however, clearly flows from ownership of property. Under various reasonable assumptions, it is possible to allocate noncorporate entrepreneurial income to the more fundamental categories of "wages and salaries" and "property." In the following table, we present the share of total income arising from property during the period 1900–1963. Our estimates are simply the arithmetic average of three sets of estimates reported in Table 1, page 134, of Irving B. Kravis, "Income Distribution" in *International Encyclopedia of the Social Sciences*, ed. David L. Sills (New York: Macmillan, 1968).

Period[a]	Property's Share of Total Income (percent)
1900–1909	31.6
1910–1919	34.4
1920–1929	28.8
1930–1939	21.4
1939–1948	24.4
1949–1958	23.0
1954–1963	21.2

[a]Comparative estimates allocating 25 percent of entrepreneurial income to the property share are given for 1955–1957 and 1965–1967 (24.6 percent and 24.7 percent, respectively) by Pryor, *Property and Industrial Organization* (page 72).

7. Although there are data for more recent years and concerning roughly the same issue, these data have some special limitations. First, they do not deal with standardized categories such as income fifths and so their usefulness for comparative purposes is limited. Second, they refer to tax returns and so are conservative reports of income in general and of certain types of income in particular. The best example of such data known to us and useful as a supplement to the data we have reported is that given by Frank Ackerman et al., "Income Distribution in the United States," *Review of Radical Political Economics* 3 (Summer 1971): 20–43. We have reproduced for the reader two tables from this article that give the distribution over broad income classes of the major types of income and the distribution over type within each of the classes. These are Tables A1 and A2.

8. See, for example, the data from Ackerman et al., "Income Distribution in the United States."

APPENDIX

Table A1 Income Levels by Type of Income on 1966 Tax Returns

Size of Taxable Income	Tax Returns (percent)	All Types (percent)	Type of Income[a]			
			Wage and Salary (percent)	Entrepreneurial (percent)	Property (percent)	Other (percent)
Under $20,000	97.3	83.9	91.6	61.8	37.6	62.2
$20,000–50,000	2.3	10.0	6.5	26.1	21.4	20.3
$50,000–100,000	.3	3.2	1.4	8.8	13.5	9.5
Over $100,000	.1	2.8	.5	3.2	27.5	8.1
Totals	100.0	99.9	100.0	99.9	100.0	100.1
(billions of dollars)	—	478.2	381.1	56.8	32.7	7.4

Source: Adapted from Table 6, page 27, Frank Ackerman et al., "Income Distribution in the United States," *Review of Radical Political Economics* 3, 3(Summer 1971):20–43.

[a]"Entrepreneurial" income consists of interest, rent, and income of farmers, unincorporated businesses, proprietors, and self-employed professionals. "Property" income consists of dividends and capital gains. Obviously, entrepreneurial income is unallocated income from labor or property.

Table A2 Types of Income Within Income Levels on 1966 Tax Returns

Size of Taxable Income	All Types	Types of Income (percent of all types)			
		Wage and Salary	Entrepreneurial	Property	Other
Under $20,000	100.0	87.0	8.8	3.1	1.1
$20,000–50,000	100.0	51.4	30.8	14.6	3.2
$50,000–100,000	100.0	34.4	32.5	28.6	4.5
Over $100,000	100.0	15.6	13.3	66.7	4.4
Total	100.0	79.7	11.9	6.8	1.6

Source: Adapted from Tables 5 and 6, pages 27–28, Frank Ackerman et al., "Income Distribution in the United States," *Review of Radical Political Economics* 3, 3(Summer 1971):20–43.

4
UNDERSTANDING
INEQUALITY

From our detailed analysis of wealth and income distribution in America, it is clear that a considerable amount of inequality exists. Although the data are in many ways incomplete, they form a sufficiently precise picture to raise the questions: Why is there so much inequality? What forces perpetuate this system of resource distribution?

In searching for answers to these questions, we would do well to recall the elementary principles of inequality enumerated in Chapter 1: (1) The existence of economic surplus creates distributive problems; (2) conditioned by thousands of years of struggle for survival, humans compete for shares of the surplus; (3) those who have won in this competition are able to buy power that can be used to preserve privilege; (4) to decrease the need for the use of coercion, those with power seek to mitigate conflicts of interest by the use of ideas.

SOCIAL STRUCTURE AND INEQUALITY

These elementary principles are too elementary. But they do provide guidelines for examining the social structures that perpetuate inequality in America. The existence of economic surplus and the distribution problems it creates should alert us to the economics of inequality. Preliterate and modern industrial economies perform essentially the same functions of extracting resources from the environment, converting them into usable goods, and then distributing valuable goods and services to the members of society. The scale and scope of such basic economic processes vary enormously from society to society, but the nature of the basic processes remains unaltered. Just as was surely true of the first preliterate societies, then, patterns of inequality in the United States reflect the amount of available surplus and the nature of the competitive struggles among economic participants to secure shares of this surplus.

As we have emphasized, winners in the competition for surplus can acquire power to perpetuate inequality in the access to surplus. It should be recognized, of course, that social life is not quite this simple. Nevertheless, it is not too much of an oversimplification to argue that the history of human societies is a chronicle of how economic elites have sought to consolidate their power into governments that could in turn regulate economic processes so as to perpetuate their privileged position. The institution of government is a seat of power in society. Thus, an analysis of government is critical to understanding how regulation of economic processes is selective and results in the perpetuation of patterns of inequality among different segments of a society.

In the United States, the economy was relatively unregulated by government during the early period of industrialization. Those who came to own much of the economic surplus were able to disproportionately influence the way the government began to intervene in economic affairs. As we demonstrate in later chapters, this unequal influence is likely to occur regardless of the degree of political democracy considered to exist in a society. Thus, political decisions in a society, especially those involving the regulation of the economy, reflect disproportionately the interests of those segments of the society that have money to buy power. The word *disproportionate* is important, for we are not arguing that an economic-political elite has ever controlled, or even today controls, all decision making in America. Such a contention would be obviously false, although some do not agree that this assertion is obvious.[1] The poor and the middle-income groupings exert a considerable amount of power, *but not proportionate to their numbers.* Moreover, the privileged few have used their power to divide the middle- and lower-income groupings. One result of this use of power is that the middle classes of America inadvertently support the privilege of elites, although in the long run their self-interest is served by alliance with those they misperceive as the enemy—the impoverished and those on "the welfare dole."

With the middle-income groupings diverted, the privileged have been able to exert political influence that has created a political *wealth*fare system. This wealthfare system affects privilege both directly and indirectly. The wealthfare system directly maintains privilege, either by allowing the wealthy to avoid taxation of their income and wealth or by bestowing on them direct cash payments and subsidies. This system indirectly preserves privilege by giving various forms of subsidy to those economic organizations owned and operated by the wealthy, thereby increasing the income and assets the wealthy can derive from the economy. It is, largely, through the wealthfare system that economic elites now maintain their privilege. The middle-income groups perceive this wealthfare system as preserving *their* affluence, but this perception is often inaccurate. This system does little except allow the rich to preserve their privilege with the active cooperation of the vast majority.

In contrast to the wealthfare system is the welfare system. Welfare in America is reluctantly implemented and is the subject of much commentary, debate, and hatred, especially by middle-income groupings. The reasons for a welfare system are varied: (1) it is necessary to keep people from starving; (2) it is defined as humanitarian; (3) it is politically necessary because the poor have some power, especially when they threaten to revolt; and (4) it is an effective way for the rich to keep the attention of the majority diverted away from the much more expensive *wealth*fare system.

The welfare system actually operates to perpetuate poverty, and it can be viewed as a reflection of the low degree of power possessed by disadvantaged economic groups. As with the wealthfare system, the perpetuation of poverty is accomplished both directly and indirectly. The welfare system keeps direct payments low, usually just below established subsistence levels. And the welfare system both induces and forces the poor to work in *any* available job, thus indirectly keeping people poor by making them take employment in marginal and low paying jobs.

In sum, then, it is our basic hypothesis that economic inequality leads to the consolidation of different degrees of political power and the creation of a dual welfare and wealthfare system by government. Those with economic resources—that is, those who have been successful in their dealings within the economy—have money, organization, and the capacity to develop contacts with political decision makers. In fact, at times they are the political decision makers. The end result is for those with money to consolidate power, or at the very least, disproportionately influence those who actually hold the power. Because they have power and influence, economic elites can assure that a disproportionate number of political decisions will benefit them. In contrast, those without resources have little power and, hence, little ability to influence political decisions in their favor. These differences in political power of the privileged and poor are maintained by a dual system of welfare and wealthfare. And it is this dual system that maintains inequality in America. In Figure 1, we have outlined diagrammatically the key relationships among the economy, polity, and welfare-wealthfare systems on the one hand and a system of privilege and poverty on the other.

Figure 1 represents an outline or table of contents for the remaining chapters of this book. Further, it can be viewed as a diagrammatic outline of how elementary principles of inequality might operate in a complex society like the United States. The key relationship in Figure 1 is between the economy and polity. Those who control economic arrangements exert disproportionate political power. This exertion of power has, over time, become institutionalized into a dual wealthfare and welfare system, as

Figure 1 Key Structural Arrangements and Inequality in America

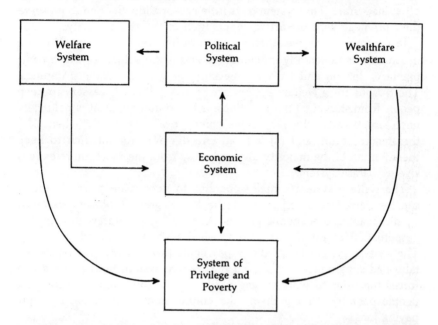

is indicated by the arrows in the figure. And finally, as the arrows indicate, the existence of this dual system operates directly, and indirectly through the economy, to perpetuate a system of privilege and poverty in America.

The brief discussion of elementary principles of inequality in preliterate societies indicates that structural arrangements promoting inequality do not operate in a cultural vacuum; they are usually justified and legitimated by ideas. It can be hypothesized that the greater the economic surplus and the more unequal its distribution, then the greater the reliance on ideas to convince the less privileged of the rightness of the existing system. There is both enormous surplus and vast inequality in the United States, and we now direct our analytical attention to understanding the nature of idea systems in America and how those systems are used to legitimate inequality.

CULTURE AND INEQUALITY
In America, the middle classes, and even many in the poverty categories have traditionally accepted structural arrangements that promote inequality. Many Americans grumble and complain about inequality and inequity, and revolts and riots have underscored the frustration of some deprived segments of the society. But direct challenges to the welfare and wealthfare systems have been surprisingly rare in the face of enormous inequality. The analysis of any set of stable structural relations thus raises the question: Why have they been perceived as legitimate by the majority over most of American history? Structural arrangements

are not maintained by coercion alone, although we would not want to underestimate the use of force in America; but to paraphrase the reactionary Edmund Burke, "no nation is ruled which must be perpetually conquered." Coercion has been used frequently in recent years to oppress protesting students and urban poor. But the welfare and wealthfare systems have remained intact because they are legitimated by ideas that are shared collectively by large segments of the American population.

The proliferation of complex patterns of social organization would not be possible without the capacity of humans to utilize and elaborate symbols into systems of ideas. Ideas are what make humans unique, for no other species appears capable of regulating its conduct by values, beliefs, ideologies, scientific doctrines, religious dogmas, technologies, and other systems of symbols. Ideas can be defined as symbols that have been *organized* into coherent *systems of information* utilized by members of a population to *guide and regulate their perception and conduct.*

For example, the simultaneous occurrence of ideas emphasizing progress through technology and knowledge about how to manipulate the environment greatly accelerated industrialization of medieval Europe and brought high levels of material comfort. Ideas therefore have a profound impact on the ways humans build and elaborate social structures; and conversely, ideas are created by humans actively confronting each other and the problems of their existence. This reciprocity between ideas and social structure indicates that the analysis of one cannot exclude attention to the other. Ideas arise from the activities of humans, but once created they feed back on these activities and affect their subsequent course.

The concept of *ideas* is extremely abstract and embraces many different *types* of symbol systems affecting human action in *different* ways. Which systems of ideas are most important in understanding inequality in general and specifically in the United States? For our purposes, two types of ideas, and the interrelationships among them, are considered most critical: (1) values and (2) beliefs.[2] As will be emphasized, each of these types of ideas represents, by itself, an *organization* of symbols into a *system.* Equally important, there are clear linkages between systems of values and beliefs, because each is part of a larger system of ideas.

Values[3]

As one *type* of idea, values involve the organization of symbols that have implications for what people perceive and what they do in their social relations. But this broad formulation needs to be clarified if the concept is to be distinguished from other idea systems and to be useful in understanding inequality. Common sense observations on values provide an initial basis for narrowing the definition.

First, most observers recognize that to discuss values is to engage in a discourse on *abstract principles* drawn from people's experiences in everyday life. Second, such abstract principles are *emotionally charged,* for they are capable of mobilizing human emotions and conduct. Third, values reveal an individual's conceptions of *what is desirable*. And finally, most would agree that values have implications for *how people behave*.

These commonly agreed upon observations come very close to providing a formal definition of values, as utilized in sociological theory and research. To translate formally: *Values are those highly general and abstract conceptions that are held by members of a population and that provide the criteria for defining and assessing desirable conduct.* As such, values provide the standards by which members of a population evaluate their own conduct and that of others. Although these standards often guide and regulate behavior and are therefore an important source of social control in social systems, many other forces shape human action. Thus, the fit between the values of a population and the behavior of its members, as well as their organization into various social patterns, is never perfect. However, it would be impossible to understand the operation of human society without also comprehending the organization of values that, however imperfectly, provide the criteria for assessing desirable conduct.

Beliefs[4]

In one of its everyday usages, the concept of *belief* pertains to what people believe in, as when a person believes in God. Another common sense definition of belief focuses on people's opinions about social phenomena, as when one believes that all welfare recipients are lazy. These two common sense formulations come close to the sociological definition of the concept of beliefs, because they point to beliefs as conceptions about *what exists*. However, people also hold beliefs about *what should be*. For example, one can believe that capitalism should be allowed to flourish unregulated and that welfare loafers should be put to work. Thus, our definition must take into account that belief systems contain conceptions about what is and what should be.

How do beliefs differ from values? First, beliefs are much less abstract and refer to *concrete* people, groups, events, and situations, whereas values represent abstract conceptions transcending any particular situation, event, or person. Second, unlike values, beliefs do not provide criteria or standards for assessing desirable and undesirable conduct; rather, they indicate what exists or what should be, without providing the standards or criteria to support such beliefs. Beliefs do not reveal why something should be, only that a particular and concrete state of affairs should exist.

It is now possible to offer a more formal definition of beliefs. *Beliefs are concrete conceptions that are held by members of a population and that reveal their understandings about what exists in particular settings and their feelings about what the state of affairs should be in a particular setting.* As such, two general types of beliefs can be discerned: (1) *evaluative beliefs* pertaining to concrete conceptions of what should exist in a specified setting; and

(2) *empirical beliefs* referring to concrete concepts about what actually exists in a particular setting.

Systems of Values and Beliefs

The values of a society tend to be organized into a system, as do beliefs and other components of culture. Discrete values and beliefs do not stand alone. Rather, they reveal an affinity or consistency with other beliefs or values. However, as the vagueness of *affinity* and *consistency* underscores, the nature of interrelations among either values or beliefs is not clearly understood, nor is it a simple task to study their interrelations. These observations perhaps render premature, or even incorrect, the assertion that beliefs and values are organized into systems. This latter position takes on even greater credence when the critic of the systems viewpoint points out marked inconsistencies and contradictions in the beliefs and values of a society. And yet, despite our limited ability to conceptualize or empirically examine values or beliefs as systems, the consistencies and compatibilities among values far outweigh the inconsistencies. And the apparent affinity of individual components makes the conceptualization of idea systems highly appealing. Thus, for our *purposes of analysis*, values and beliefs of a society will be visualized as comprising an imperfectly integrated system. As a system, ideas influence action in concert, since the content of one compelling idea invokes that of other ideas. It is in this way, then, that congeries of ideas simultaneously shape human action.

While values and beliefs constitute separable systems, they represent only two types of ideas, and it is likely that they represent only two subsystems of a more encompassing idea system. Again, many would argue against this conclusion by pointing to contradictions between values and beliefs and by challenging us to demonstrate in both conceptual and concrete empirical terms the linkages between these subsystems. Hopefully, we will be able to provide some evidence in support of this position, but for the moment, it is argued that: (1) values and beliefs represent separable subsystems of an overall idea system; (2) these two subsystems bear organized relations to each other; and (3) this organization is hierarchical, with values representing more abstract conceptualizations than beliefs and, within belief systems, evaluative beliefs representing more abstract formulations than empirical beliefs.[5]

From this perspective, values provide the abstract criteria for assessing desirable and undesirable conduct, while evaluative beliefs apply these criteria to specific settings in a society by postulating what should be. In turn, empirical beliefs are greatly circumscribed by evaluative beliefs, because conceptions of what exists in the social world are always filtered through the prism of what individuals believe should exist. However, because conceptions of what is and what exists are influenced by the experiences and observations of people as they cope with concrete situations, it would be expected that, in any society, empirical beliefs will deviate considerably from either values or evaluative beliefs. But as we will document, the sometimes spectacular inaccuracy of empirical beliefs gives a rough indication of the extent to which evaluative beliefs, as representations of abstract values, determine what individuals perceive to exist in the world around them.

In Figure 2, these hierarchical relations among values, evaluative beliefs, and empirical beliefs are diagrammed. The arrows flowing downward indicate that evaluative beliefs are influenced by values and that, in turn, empirical beliefs are partial reflections of evaluative beliefs. The arrow pointing to social structural arrangements underscores our assumption that people behave and act upon empirical beliefs, even though these can be inaccurate and, at times, contradictory of evaluative beliefs. This assumption has profound implications for the analysis of why the American pattern of inequality has remained so stable, as is emphasized by the arrows connecting structural arrangements and the system of privilege and poverty. The arrows flowing upward from social structural arrangements emphasize that ideas are connected to social structure and have important consequences for regulating institutional arrangements only so long as they are capable of justifying and legitimating these arrangements. When social structures change, people's empirical beliefs are altered, with the result that, over time, changes in evaluative beliefs are likely to occur. And eventually, if the social structural changes are sufficiently extensive and enduring to make evaluative beliefs highly incompatible with values, then alterations in the system of values of a society can be expected.

As Figure 2 underscores, then, the institutional arrangements in the economy and polity that perpetuate inequality are not only justified and legitimated by the ideas of culture but are to a great extent regulated and guided by these ideas. However, much of what occurs in society is unregulated by ideas, because conflicts among interest groups, the coercive use of power, and the deceptive manipulation of individuals are pervasive phenomena. And yet, even in these seemingly noncultural structural processes, it is evident that values and beliefs are often used to mobilize individuals into conflict groupings, to legitimate physical coercion, or to provide the basis for deceptive manipulation of individuals. These complex relations between American culture and society, however, represent a more detailed story that is told in subsequent chapters.

Dominant Values and Inequality

Just as it is necessary to offer a preliminary outline of how key structural arrangements in the economy and government maintain inequality, so it is desirable to offer a brief summary of dominant American values. These values provide the legitimating premises for beliefs and structural arrangements. In later chapters we seek to connect these value premises

Figure 2 Systems of Values and Beliefs

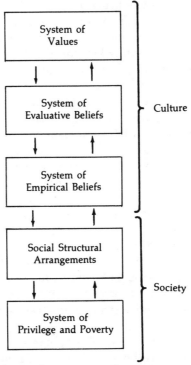

to beliefs and to the key social structures that preserve the system of privilege and poverty. Here we will argue that, to comprehend the structural forces that maintain inequality, at least nine components of America's value system[6] need to be outlined: (1) *activism*, (2) *achievement*, (3) *progress*, (4) *materialism*, (5) *freedom*, (6) *individualism*, (7) *egalitarianism*, (8) *morality*, and (9) *humanitarianism*. These nine values are assumed to represent a system in that each provides criteria for assessing the desirability of the others. For example, to say that one values freedom is to say only that action should be unrestrained by external forces—the units, activities, and situations that are to go unregulated are not described. This missing information is supplied by other values, such as individualism. In this particular case, individualism emphasizes that it is the individual person who is to be free from external constraints. In turn, other values provide additional criteria for assessing desirable action by free individuals, and so on as values reciprocally provide criteria for assessing desirable and appropriate action.

Activism.[7] This value emphasizes the desirability and appropriateness of shaping, controlling, and manipulating the world by intense effort or activity. Further, this effort at control and manipulation should be rational and directed toward the accurate assessment of the best means to achieve clearly understood goals and purposes. Just what should constitute the best means is influenced by considerations of practicality and efficiency. In other words, little motion should be wasted in achieving goals, and activity should involve efforts at resolving practical or immediately present problems. In America, then, much action is assessed in terms of the energy expended in the rational and efficient pursuit of practical goals, because this kind of activity is considered most likely to facilitate control and manipulation of the environment.

Achievement. Not only should activity lead to control, it should also allow actors to do well in competition with each other. In particular, it is considered desirable to achieve—that is, to do well—in important institutional spheres. Such achievement should, however, be fairly and decently accomplished.

Materialism. Efforts at achievement and success are to be directed toward increasing people's levels of material comfort and their capacity to cultivate leisure time. Thus, in American society, the winners in competition should be able to display their success through the consumption of material goods and the utilization of leisure time.

Progress. Activity directed at controlling and achieving is considered to lead in America to the betterment of the individual and the society. That is, the changes wrought by efforts to control the world and achieve material comfort will be directional, and cumulatively they will allow both the individual and society to progress to a higher level than previously possible.

Freedom. If activity is to result in progress, it should go unrestrained by external forces. Although all social life must to some extent be constrained, it is critical that as much social action as possible be free of excessive constraints. Otherwise, action cannot be rational or efficient, nor can it allow actors to realize the full extent of their achievements.

Individualism. Freedom from external constraint is particularly critical for individuals who, in the end, are the actors responsible for achievement and progress. While larger social units, such as corporations, should also enjoy minimal constraints, it is most important for individuals to be allowed full and unconstrained opportunity to achieve material success and prosperity through their efforts.

Egalitarianism.[8] Freedom for individuals should promote a democracy in which each individual has an equal opportunity to achieve. Forces that impede such equal opportunity should be eliminated, because they violate each individual's right to be free of external consraint.

Morality. Activities are to be judged as right or wrong. Although not all activity is easily assessed, it is desirable to seek judgments as to the rightness or wrongness of each individual's efforts. Such efforts at establishing the morality of actions are to utilize the standards of desirability that have persisted over the decades in American society (that is, the above values).

Humanitarianism. Those who have achieved material comfort through their efforts should be charitable to those less fortunate and in need.

But charity cannot be unconditional, for only those who are unable to be active in the American system, or those who have fallen upon misfortune in their activities within the system, are deserving of assistance from those who have received its benefits and rewards.

As should be obvious in this brief portrayal of dominant American values, we have simplified, and perhaps oversimplified, a very complex phenomenon. However, it is this interrelated cluster of values that now supports the welfare and wealthfare systems perpetuating inequality. Even this simplified portrait enables us to visualize the many ways values regulate, legitimate, and justify the pattern of inequality in the United States.

Why do these values exist? One answer is too simple: These values exist because they promote the privilege of those who derive most of the wealth. There is some validity to this hypothesis, for the wealthy and the powerful do utilize these values to manipulate the population and justify the privileges. But values emerge through complex historical processes and only some are related to the present interests of powerful economic groups. In the United States, some of these values were apparently imported by the original colonists and became the basis for organizing communal and religious activities. The emphases on the individual, morality, freedom, achievement, efficient activity, and material charity are all, to some extent, reflections of the Puritan Ethic common to the early Protestant colonists, many of whom came to America to escape persecution. The profile of these values was certainly altered by the comparatively unregulated opportunities that individuals perceived to exist in a frontier society. And then, coupled with rapid industrialization and the prosperity generated by early capitalism in America, these values were further altered into their current profile.

It is, of course, beyond the scope of this short book to trace the historical development of the American system of values.[9] What is important for our purposes is to recognize that any system of values is inherited from past generations, and that even when such inherited values no longer are compatible with new structural arrangements, they persist for a time and provide standards for people's evaluations of each other. Values persist for many reasons: (1) because they are passed down from generation to generation through socialization; (2) because they support and justify at least some structural arrangements; (3) because humans are complex, symbol-using creatures who have an amazing capacity to tolerate, segregate, and isolate inconsistencies; and (4) because powerful groups can use any accepted value to manipulate a population in order to preserve the groups' privileges. And so it is with this profile of American values. They are the products of historical and contemporary forces that are only vaguely understood. We seek to demonstrate how these values operate and how they are used by various groups to perpetuate inequality in the United States.

SUMMARY AND PREVIEW

Inequality is maintained by powerful social and cultural forces that form a complex web of interrelations. We have yet to unravel the strands of this web and examine them in detail, but the basic profile of our argument should now be clear. Economic arrangements create groupings with different degrees of political power, and these groupings have created a dual welfare and wealthfare system in America. This dual system is legitimated by dominant values, especially as these have been elaborated into specific belief systems.

This portrayal is an application of elementary principles of inequality to a concrete society, the United States. And as such, our portrayal represents only tentative guidelines for understanding inequality in America and for developing a more mature theory of inequality in modern social systems.

This overall framework is outlined in Figure 3, which is intended to be both a summary of our discussion thus far and a preview of how we will approach the analysis of inequality in America.

As Figure 3 underscores, we will argue that understanding of the cultural forces legitimating the political, welfare, and wealthfare systems

Figure 3 The Sociocultural Basis of Inequality

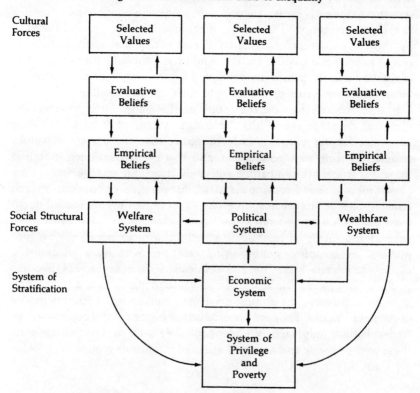

is critical to understanding both the direct and indirect processes that maintain privilege and poverty. Various empirical beliefs will be seen to distort perceptions about the welfare, political, and wealthfare systems, because those with power have been able to *disproportionately* (not completely) influence the selection of the dominant values that have become codified into evaluative beliefs about welfare, wealthfare, and political decision-making. It is this web among values, beliefs, and structural arrangements that perpetuates privilege and poverty in America and makes the profile of inequality outlined in Chapters 2 and 3 difficult to alter.

NOTES

1. The first well-articulated assertion along these lines was formulated by C. Wright Mills in *The Power Elite* (New York: Oxford, 1956).

2. As will become evident, this discussion draws heavily from Talcott Parsons, *The Social System* (New York: Free Press, 1951), pp. 326–384. Hopefully, the almost reflexive criticisms of those who acknowledge a debt to Parsons will be suspended until we have been able to complete our analysis. Also, see: Clyde Kluckhohn, "Values and Value-Orientations in the Theory of Action: An Exploration in Definition and Classification," in *Toward a General Theory of Action*, ed. Talcott Parsons and Edward A. Shils (Cambridge, Mass.: Harvard University Press, 1951), pp. 388–433.

3. The following discussion draws on several sources, the most important of which are: Robin M. Williams, Jr., "Values," in *International Encyclopedia of the Social Sciences*, vol. 16, ed. David L. Sills (New York: Macmillan, 1968), pp. 283–287; Robin M. Williams, Jr., *American Society: A Sociological Interpretation*, 3rd ed. (New York: Alfred Knopf, 1970), pp. 438–451; Milton Rokeach, *The Nature of Human Values* (New York: Macmillan, 1973), pp. 3–25; Milton Rokeach, *Beliefs, Attitudes and Values* (San Francisco: Jossey-Bass, 1968); and Florence Kluckhohn and Fred L. Strodtbeck, *Variations in Value Orientations* (Evanston, Ill.: Row, Peterson, 1961).

4. We have been influenced heavily in this discussion by Rokeach, *Beliefs, Attitudes, and Values*; Joan Huber and William H. Form, *Income and Ideology: An Analysis of the American Political Formula* (New York: Free Press, 1973), pp. 1–61; Karl Manheim, *Ideology and Utopia* (New York: Harcourt, Brace, 1936).

5. Obviously, we are attempting to utilize Talcott Parsons' concept of the "cybernetic hierarchy of control" in the analysis of inequality. See, for example, Parsons' "An Outline of the Social System," in *Theories of Society*, ed. Talcott Parsons et al., (New York: Free Press, 1961).

6. This discussion represents a reworking of the values delineated in Williams' *American Society*, pp. 452–500.

7. We have subsumed, under the value complex of "activism," Williams' discussion of "efficiency" and "practicality" as separate values.

8. We have collapsed Williams' separate classification of the values "equality" and "democracy" under one value complex, "egalitarianism."

9. For some excellent discussions of values in American history, particularly as they pertain to inequality, see: Neil Betten, "American Attitudes Toward the Poor: A Historical Overview," *Current History*, 65 (July 1973): 1–5; Dorothy Buckton James, *Poverty, Politics, and Change* (Englewood Cliffs, N.J.: Prentice-Hall, 1972), pp. 21–72; Ben Seligman, *Permanent Poverty: An American Syndrome* (Chicago: Quadrangle Books, 1970): Clyde Kluckhohn, "Have There Been Discernible Shifts in American Values During the Past Generation," in *The American Style*, ed. Elting E. Morison (New York: Harper and Row, 1958); James H. Tufts, *America's Social Morality* (New York: Holt, Rinehart and Winston, 1933); and Robert H. Bremner, *From the Depths: The Discovery of Poverty in the United States* (New York: New York University Press, 1956).

5
INEQUALITY
AND POWER

The wealth and income inequalities described in Chapters 2 and 3 exist because those with wealth have the capacity to disproportionately influence political decisions. Such influence is an indicator of their power. Although revolutions, wars, and other disruptive events have at times in the histories of many societies redistributed power and other resources, virtually all known societies have revealed a system of resource and asset inequality paralleling the unequal distribution of power. The poor always pose a threat of civil disorder, and when their numbers are large and the political system somewhat democratic, they also have some voting power. Thus, the lower-income groups are never powerless. But their political organization does not place them on an equal footing with more affluent groupings.

In the United States, economic inequalities have created differences in power within a highly democratized political system. The inequalities of power have led to the creation of the wealthfare and welfare states that perpetuate economic inequalities among the poor, affluent, and wealthy. The operation of these two states or establishments requires extensive analysis. But it is necessary, first, to understand how the structure and culture of government has been selectively influenced by different economic groups.

THE CULTURE OF POLITICS IN AMERICA
Enduring structural arrangements in a society are legitimated by dominant values and beliefs. Political relations within government and between government and the pressure groupings of the poor, affluent, and

rich are thus legitimated by a complex system of ideas. The post-Watergate era has made Americans more skeptical of traditional political arrangements and supporting ideas, but the basic profile of values and beliefs as well as the political system they support have not undergone profound change.

To gain even a tentative understanding of America's political culture it is necessary to review those values that provide criteria for assessing what is desirable in the political arena. The values of activity and achievement encourage competitive efforts in the political process by individuals and groups vying for success and control of political decisions. The values of freedom and equalitarianism require an absence of excessive external constraint in this competitive activity and a guarantee that it is fair and open to all. Under conditions of freedom and equality, it is assumed that the will of the people will influence major political decisions. Thus, the most desirable constraints are those that give all individuals and groups an equal chance to compete in the political process. The value of individualism places enormous emphasis on individual competition, as opposed to group combat, in contests for political power.

These values provide abstract criteria for *evaluative beliefs* that dictate what *should* exist in the concrete political processes of a society. In the United States, evaluative beliefs appear to revolve around a concern for what can be termed a *candidate democracy* in which individual candidates, as opposed to well-organized parties, are the center of competition for political office. These beliefs are clearly evident in local community and county elections, where political parties are less important than the solvency, charisma, and other characteristics of candidates. At the state and federal level, candidates are still more important than party affiliations. A tightly-knit party does not necessarily choose its candidate; rather, candidates vie in relatively open competition for popular support among the rank and file of the party. As many commentators have noted, party organization and unity in America are loose and form as much around the platforms of popular candidates as around that of the party.

In a society that values free competition among individuals who have equal chances to be politically active, the evaluative belief that candidate-oriented elections are the best form of democracy is appropriate. Americans are distrustful of tight political organization that violates values of individualism, freedom, and equalitarianism. The capacity of many individual candidates, through their active campaign efforts, to win elections with votes from members of other parties, when coupled with the evaluative belief that this should happen, appears to have created a set of *empirical beliefs* that candidate democracies are the most representative and responsive to the problems of the people. This belief can be stated in simplified form. If individuals are allowed to freely compete with each other over the issues that affect peoples' lives, then the cause of democracy is served.

Much of the disillusionment of Watergate appears to have been caused by the recognition that this empirical belief is contradicted by the actual facts of political life. Competition among individuals is not always open, nor does it always reflect the interests of the common people. Interestingly, the reaction to Watergate has been not only withdrawal from the political process, but also a closer scrutiny of individual candidates and their affiliations with organized interests, including political parties. Such a reaction reaffirms basic values and evaluative beliefs, while indicating that Americans still hold to the empirical belief that candidate democracy is the most representative.

America's political culture has been created by forces in the political economy, while at the same time legitimating these forces. These beliefs operate rather effectively, even in the post-Watergate era, to legitimate a political system that is differentially responsive to diverse economic interests. The poor receive few favorable political decisions, the affluent receive just enough to keep them comparatively content, and the wealthy receive many that preserve their privileges. To understand just how these values and beliefs operate in the political arena, we must turn our attention to some key features of governmental structure in America.

INEQUALITY AND THE ELECTION OF POLITICAL DECISION MAKERS

Democratic forms of government, such as we have in the United States, develop mechanisms for letting the population, directly or indirectly, place incumbents in key political decision-making positions. In contrast to many modern democracies, party organization in America is comparatively loose. Although national candidates seek party affiliation and rely on party resources, it is the candidate as much as the party who raises funds and it is the candidate's policies and programs that usually determine how people vote. This loose party organization is supported by dominant values and beliefs. Such a system allows for close scrutiny of internal party processes, but it makes the political processes highly vulnerable to influence by the wealthy.

Because candidates must often campaign in primaries to win party nomination, they must seek funding for two political contests, the primary and the general election. In a media-dominated society where candidates must impress the public with their *unique* qualifications (above and beyond political party affiliation), political contests are expensive. Thus, to the extent that candidates must be distinguished from party policies, each candidate must seek financial assistance both within and outside of his party. Such a system is legitimated, and made necessary, by dominant values and beliefs that require candidates to give the impression that they are "their own men" and that their individual records are as important as their party's.

To become an incumbent and to maintain this incumbency, then, requires extensive financing. Such financial assistance is most easily afforded by organized interests and the wealthy. Campaign reporting laws will make this more evident, but, they are unlikely to negate the political reality of campaign financing. As long as party goals are vague and organization is loose, and as long as only two parties dominate, candidate democracy, and the financial burden it places on candidates, will prevail.

There has been some indication recently that candidates can win elections with large numbers of small campaign contributions. But this pattern has not prevailed traditionally and is not a clear trend even today. It is difficult to assess at present whether public financing of state and congressional elections will become a real alternative to large contributions from small numbers of wealthy supporters. Thus, the result of a candidate democracy, in a media-dominated society without strong parties and without public financing of campaigns, is that the wealthy and the organizations of the affluent have more influence on candidates and incumbents than do the less affluent and the poor.

The elective process in America must be viewed, then, as one source of inequality. By itself, such a process might not be too damaging. Indeed, a candidate democracy has many advantages over a multiple party democratic system. But the structuring of the federal government in the United States reinforces the biases built into the election process.

INEQUALITY AND THE STRUCTURE OF THE FEDERAL GOVERNMENT
The Federalist Structure and Inequality
The national government is divided into three branches, the executive, the congressional, and the judicial. At the state, county, and local community levels this tripartite division of political decision-making is paralleled by various judicial, elective, and administrative agencies. One of the basic problems of this structure is the coordination of national programs among community, county, state, and federal branches of government. Buttressed by *states rights* and *local control and autonomy*—evaluative beliefs, which reflect the more general value of *freedom*—state governments frequently seek to maintain autonomy from the national government. In turn, county governments often try to maintain a base of power that is separate from state government, and local communities usually attempt to maintain decision-making boundaries between each other and between city and county governments.

One result of this overall political structure is that the delivery of services from the national government to state, county, and local governments is difficult. Conflicts between various levels of government inevitably force awkward and wasteful administrative procedures. Nowhere is this awkwardness more evident than in the delivery of welfare to the poor, because federal, state, and county governments must coordinate their activities. Such a structure has made the delivery of welfare services not only costly but often inefficient and sometimes inhumane to welfare clients.

This same structure would obstruct effective administration of more extensive income redistribution programs. For example, administration of an adequate guaranteed annual income from direct expenditures by the federal government would pose problems. How would the money be disbursed to those in need? Should the state, county, or city government be involved? Or should an entirely new set of national agencies be established? If this were done, what would be the new function of existing state, county, and city agencies? There are no simple answers to these questions, which underscore the structural barriers to effective national programs of income redistribution. However, these barriers are at present unlikely to be encountered, because the political decisions to redistribute income at the federal level of government are not likely to be made.

The Structure of Congress and Inequality

Because virtually all legislation affecting welfare and wealthfare must pass through Congress, the structure of this decision-making body becomes critical to maintenance of the present systems of privilege and poverty. It is clear that welfare and wealthfare reform will require extensive *national* and *change-oriented* legislation from Congress, and yet the structure of Congress is currently not suited for effective national and change-oriented legislation. Several of its features help account for this situation:

(1) Because the election process is dominated by the media and is expensive, candidates must seek financial backing from many organizations that currently benefit from the status quo. As a result, many senators and congressmen are reluctant to vote for new reform-oriented national legislation that would conflict with the interests of at least some of their financial backers. Although the backers of a representative or a senator may often have conflicts of interest among themselves, they can sometimes form a *de facto* coalition against any comprehensive piece of national legislation that would result in widespread social change and could potentially disrupt each of their unique interests. As is often true, the major financial backers of candidates and decision-makers may have little in common except their opposition to legislation that would change a system from which they all derive privilege. It is not necessary to impute a conspiracy to the financial elites, although at times one may exist. It is only necessary to recognize the natural tendency of the privileged to resist changes in the status quo. In the context of inequality, income redistribution would encounter enormous resistance from all the individuals and organizations who benefit or perceive that they benefit from the dual welfare and wealthfare system.

(2) Within Congress, all legislation must pass through the appropriate committee. Committees can pigeonhole, rewrite, stall, or kill almost any bill, and within a committee its chair has enormous power. Because committee chairs are usually selected on the basis of seniority rather than competence or expertise, they tend to come from rural areas of states, or from rural states, where interests are unambiguous, relatively unchanging, and typically conservative. In a society that is rife with conflicts of interests and undergoing rapid change, these chairs in the House and Senate are sometimes unrepresentative of the broader societal constituency and are thus less likely to be responsive to national needs. They are more likely to resist any proposed programs that would alter the current wealthfare system and redistribute resources.

Thus, the structure of Congress impedes most nationally-oriented legislation, except perhaps extremely safe items like national security and social security (although even these encounter resistance at times). Controversial measures such as income and wealth redistribution would require adjustments by large numbers of the affluent and well-financed interests, whose responses are more likely to further rigidify structural impediments to national legislation.

The Structure of the Executive Branch and Inequality

Because of his power to mold and influence opinion, the president has considerably more latitude than Congress in advocating change-oriented legislation. Of course, this legislation must eventually pass through Congress where resistance cannot always be overcome. And despite the power of the president, he cannot always ignore the sentiments of the affluent majority and the interests of financial backers who might oppose change-oriented legislation. Probably only during periods of perceived or actual crisis, when the affluent majority are dissatisfied and some large financial interests are disposed to change, can the president use his power to push comprehensive, change-oriented legislation through Congress. Welfare legislation may be passed because the public perceives a crisis to exist, but similar reform of the wealthfare system is likely to encounter enormous resistance.

All reform-oriented legislation is likely to be resisted from sources within the executive branch—the major departments and agencies comprising the administrative arm of government. The major cabinet agencies—Health, Education, and Welfare; Housing and Urban Development; Defense; Agriculture; Labor; Interior; Treasury; and Commerce—constitute, by themselves, a significant series of pressure groups whose interests could conflict with a new program for the poor. The Defense Department could be threatened by budgetary cutbacks, the Treasury Department by changes in taxing and revenue procedures, Labor by a shift in policy away from manpower training, and divisions in HEW by termination of *their* special programs. The end result of this situation would be further mobilization of pressure on Congress and the president against major alterations in the existing system of income distribution.

Thus, in summary, the current structure of the executive branch of the national government operates, in diverse and complex ways, to perpetuate inequality. Out of the interaction with public opinion and the desire to maintain power, the Office of the President and the major executive agencies typically support only minor changes in the existing system. This is particularly likely to be true of income distribution because public sentiment, economic interests, and vested interests within the executive branch would be aroused.

The Judiciary and Inequality

Perhaps as much as any branch of government, the federal court system—culminating in the United States Supreme Court—has acted to reduce inequality. For example, the reapportionment of "one man, one vote" ruling increased the voting power of minorities concentrated in the cores of large cities; the famous school desegregation decision has probably improved to some limited degree the educational opportunities of some minority poor; and the Court's rulings against welfare restrictions have certainly helped many poor.

Yet, the decisions of the Court have not, and probably cannot, affect significantly those institutional forces that maintain the existing *pattern* of inequality in America. Improvement of educational opportunities, for instance, may help some *individuals* move out of poverty classes into affluence, but it does not eliminate the economic, political, and legal forces that maintain the poverty classes. Removal of welfare restrictions may help some people avoid hardship and suffering, but it does not change the low payments to recipients. The "one man, one vote" ruling gave the poor in key urban areas some additional voting power with which to extract concessions from local, state, and federal decision-makers. But given the minority position of the poor, voting power is unlikely to create sufficient political pressure to cause income redistribution.

Thus, the capacity of the Supreme Court to rule on the constitutionality of laws and practices is unlikely to alter dramatically—at least in the foreseeable future—the regressive nature of some taxes, the loopholes in progressive taxes, the lack of economic opportunities, the low wages for unskilled jobs, or the structure of congressional and executive decision-making. And so, although the reforms initiated by the federal courts should not be underemphasized, they are not likely to cause major reorganization in the *structure* of inequality in American society.

PRESSURE GROUPINGS AND INEQUALITY

Despite cynical proclamations to the contrary, American society is highly democratized compared to other systems in the world. Democracy and equality of influence, however, are not the same thing. Democracy implies only that all segments of a population have *some degree*—not necessarily an equal degree—of influence on political decisions. Some segments of a population in any democracy are more equal than others, because they can bring more pressure to bear on governmental decision-makers than can other segments.

The number of variables that affect the capacity to exert political pressure is large, and the interactions among them are multiple and complex. Some important variables include: (1) the size of the population attempting to exert influence; (2) the distribution of this population, particularly with respect to urban and rural regions; (3) the level of organization of this population into pressure groupings; (4) the type of organization—especially its centralization, coordination, and control of members as well as of national confederations among separate organizations; (5) the financial resources available to finance the pressure activities of each organization and national confederations; (6) the existence of persuasive and widely accepted ideas—values, evaluative beliefs, and empirical beliefs—that can be used to support the programs advocated by pressure organizations; (7) the number and nature of nonsupporting ideas that would be violated by the programs advocated; (8) the length of the lobbying tradition—that is, the number of years of pressure activities—of various pressure groupings representing the interests of different income levels; and (9) the number and nature of established influence channels into various branches, departments, and offices of government.

Although data on the weights that can be assigned to these variables for different income groups are not always available, it is possible to make rough approximations about these weights for the poor (the bottom income fifth), the affluent (the middle three income fifths), and the wealthy (the top income fifth). It is likely that some poor are in the second to lowest income fifth, that the definition of affluent is very broad and encompasses very moderate income groups, and that the superwealthy probably take up only the top part of the highest income fifth. Nevertheless, it is useful for preliminary analytical purposes to distinguish the poor, the affluent, and the wealthy in terms of their differential capacity to exert political influence.

In Table 1, we have listed the nine variables on the left and the three income levels along the top. For each variable, we offer our estimates—and this is really all that they are, because few data are available—about where each income level falls with respect to these critical variables. A cursory glance at the table reveals the extent to which affluent and wealthy individuals have financial, organizational, and ideological resources available in their quest to exert political influence. In contrast, the poor have only their numbers, their incipient organizations forming loose confederations, meager financial resources, and a few supportive ideas in the struggle to exert political influence. A close examination of

Table 1 Variables Influencing Capacity to Exert Political Pressure

	The Poor (bottom income fifth)	The Affluent (middle income fifth)	The Rich (portion of top income fifth)
(1) Size of Population	large	quite large	relatively small
(2) Distribution of Population	rural and urban, large mass in cores	urban, large mass in suburbs of large cities	rural and urban, relatively high degree of dispersion
(3) Level of Organization	low, fragmented	high: unions, professional associations, corporations, and trade associations	high: corporations and trade associations
(4) Type of Organization	fragmented, decentralized, loosely coordinated national confederations	highly centralized, tightly coordinated national confederations	highly centralized, overt and covert confederations
(5) Financial Resources	meager	great	very great
(6) Supportive Ideas	value of humanitarianism and some tenets of a Welfare Ethic	Work and Welfare Ethic, national interest, trickle down	national interest, trickle down
(7) Nonsupporting Beliefs	series of unfavorable stereotypes	none	mild conflict with Work Ethic and values of activism, achievement and freedom
(8) Lobbying Tradition	short	long	long
(9) Established Influence Channels	few	many	many

the variables reveals dramatically the respective degrees of power among the poor, affluent, and wealthy.

As can be seen in Table 1, the poor and affluent represent large segments of the population. If the poor and wealthy are viewed only as falling within the upper and lowest income fifths, then their size would be equal (given the way income fifths are computed). But in actual fact, there are about thirty-five to forty million poor in America, whereas there are considerably fewer superrich (perhaps 1 million) and *highly* affluent (perhaps 20 million). The middle-income groups—the unionized blue-collar worker, the white-collar clerical and sales worker, and the highly trained professional class—constitute the largest segment of the American population who, while having different economic interests, share in America's affluence. Because the members of these middle groups derive *some* benefits from the economic system, they are often the allies of the wealthy and superwealthy who derive *enormous* benefits. They are also hesitant about approving tax increases to finance welfare and about the closing of tax loopholes from which they derive some benefit—they are suspicious of programs designed to help the poor. Further, because these middle groups represent such a large proportion of the population, political decision-makers are reluctant to initiate welfare programs and wealthfare reform that would go against the sentiments of this large constituency.

The poor are heavily massed in both rural and urban areas. Hence, much of the potential political impact of their large size is fragmented. In contrast, the middle-income groups are almost entirely situated in suburban areas of large cities or suburban communities and so have highly concentrated voting power. Although heavy concentrations of minority poor live in the core areas of large cities, this distribution has had less political impact than it would if the entire poor population were urbanized. For the wealthy, geographical distribution is less critical, because their power comes not from concentrated voting power but from their organization and financing of pressure activities.

The poor are only beginning to become politically organized. Organization of the rural poor is difficult because of their geographical dispersion, but the urban poor, particularly the black populations in the large cities, have achieved an increasing degree of organization at the *local* community level. Effective national organization, however, has not yet emerged. For the affluent, a high degree of political organization has been possible. Blue-collar workers have effective union organizations, and many white-collar employees have influential professional associations. Further, the corporations for which blue- and white-collar employees work have their own political power as well as that of various trade associations to which they belong (Chamber of Commerce, National Association of Manufacturers, and so on). The wealthy, as stockholders and high-level managers of large corporate interests, can use their corporations' lobbying force as well as their personal funds to influence political decisions. This pressure helps the wealthy, but it also assures jobs and affluence for the unionized blue-collar and professional white-collar workers who perform the economic activities that keep the rich wealthy.

The organization of the poor into pressure groupings is fragmented and decentralized. The recent emergence of the National Welfare Rights Organization (NWRO), coupled with the activities of traditional organizations such as the National Association for the Advancement of Colored People (NAACP) and other civil rights groups, gives the appearance of confederation into national pressure groups. But this level of organization is relatively ineffective when compared to that of the highly centralized unions, the large corporations, and the trade associations that represent the interests of the affluent. The wealthy also have pressure groups, but in the past those have been augmented by the capacity of the wealthy to finance, both overtly and covertly, political campaigns of decision-makers. (The impact of campaign reform laws on this activity has yet to be determined.)

The financial resources available to the poor are meager; and in fact, the organizations and activities of the poor are frequently financed by the philanthropy of the affluent and wealthy. For the affluent and wealthy, the sum total of personal, union, corporate, and trade association resources available for exerting political influence is enormous. Although corporations cannot finance political campaigns directly, they can spend money on lobbying for governmental expenditures that make profits for the owners of corporations and provide wages for the blue- and white-collar employees. The poor have no such indirect financial backing and very little direct financial leverage.

The poor have few ideological resources at their disposal. The value of humanitarianism would dictate the appropriateness of helping those in need. Similarly, the values of freedom and equalitarianism would maintain that those who are victims of discrimination should be assisted. But as we document in subsequent chapters, the values of activism, achievement, and individualism have become codified into Work and Welfare Ethics that stigmatize the poor and make them "unworthy" of excessive charity. In contrast, the Work Ethic makes the affluent seem morally entitled to their resources, because they work for their incomes. Additionally, the government's subsidy to the affluent, through contracts to economic organizations and through tax loopholes, is defined as in the "national interest" and as "trickling down" to the poor (hence making excessive welfare unnecessary). Beliefs that wealthfare is in the national interest (because it assures economic growth and societal progress) and that it trickles down to the poor (through economic expansion and the consequent creation of job opportunities) help the rich justify their wealthfare. Thus, the affluent and wealthy utilize similar beliefs to justify their respective access to resources. The poor are left with few ideological tools to justify their requests for more welfare and, more radically, for income and wealth redistribution.

Not only are the poor deprived of supporting beliefs, but dominant values and evaluative beliefs have become codified into a series of negative stereotypes (empirical beliefs) about the poor. In general, Americans regard the poor as excessively lazy and unwilling to take advantage of opportunities. The affluent are subject to few negative beliefs, because they constitute the majority and set the ideological tone of the society. The privilege of the wealthy comes into mild conflict with values of activism and achievement as codified into a Work Ethic, but their ability to hide their privilege and its sources mitigates the conflict and makes them subject to only mild suspicions from the affluent.

The poor have no lobbying tradition. Most of the little political influence exerted by the poor has developed since the 1960s, whereas the lobbying tradition of corporate interests, professional and trade associations, and labor unions is long.

This situation would indicate that formal and informal connections to members of Congress, cabinet officers heading up the executive departments of government, and even the presidency itself are extensive for the affluent and wealthy and, at best, only just emerging for the poor.

In sum, then, the poor have much less capacity to generate political pressure than do the affluent and rich. Only during periods of civil disorder have the poor exerted significant political pressure. At times, through fear, insight, and perhaps guilt, some political leaders and some heads of large organizations have acted on behalf of the poor. As we will see in Chapter 7, this pressure has provided the basis for political organization of minorities in the slums of urban areas, while allowing for rapid expansion of the welfare rolls. But it has not, and probably cannot without more developed political resources, result in any significant redistribution of either income or assets in America. Thus, one of the major institutional supports of the current system of inequality is the incapacity of the poor to exercise political pressure on the structure of government, especially when compared to the capacity of the affluent and wealthy to do so.

POWER AND INEQUALITY: AN OVERVIEW

In reviewing the structure and culture of the American political system, it is clear that values and beliefs, and the structural relations they legitimate, operate against the poor. A candidate democracy, compounded by a political structure that makes change-oriented and national decisions difficult and is subject to disproportionate pressure by the wealthy, assures a high degree of income and asset inequality. In Figure 1, we outline the key relationships between cultural and structural forces in the political system that create persistent privilege and poverty.

Figure 1 represents an elaboration of a segment or slice of the overall model presented in Chapter 3. As such, it represents our crude efforts to begin expanding on the elementary principles of inequality outlined in Chapter 1. As the arrows in Figure 1 emphasize, cultural values and beliefs bear complex reciprocal relationships with the structure of government that perpetuates inequality in the distribution of power. Our elementary principles emphasized that power differentials are often used to maintain inequality in the distribution of economic resources. And as we argued, the differences in the power of the poor, the affluent majority, and the rich have created a dual welfare and wealthfare system.

It is through this dual system that differences in power operate to perpetuate economic inequality. Our next task is to examine the specific ways that welfare and wealthfare have developed and now operate to

Figure 1

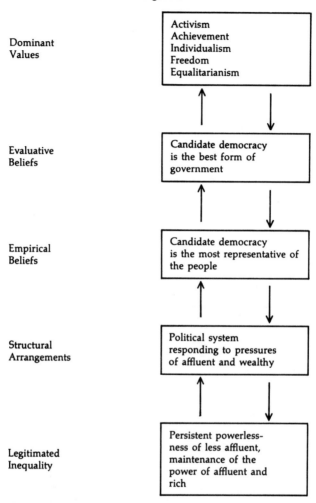

Dominant Values	Activism Achievement Individualism Freedom Equalitarianism
Evaluative Beliefs	Candidate democracy is the best form of government
Empirical Beliefs	Candidate democracy is the most representative of the people
Structural Arrangements	Political system responding to pressures of affluent and wealthy
Legitimated Inequality	Persistent powerlessness of less affluent, maintenance of the power of affluent and rich

maintain privilege and poverty. As we approach Chapters 6 and 7, it should be remembered that the welfare and wealthfare systems endure because of the political processes described in this chapter and summarized in Figure 1.

6
THE WEALTHFARE
SYSTEM
AND INEQUALITY

In this chapter, we explore the *wealth*fare system in America. It is through this system that privilege is maintained for affluent and rich individuals as well as for large corporations. Wealthfare is more difficult to analyze than welfare because it is bestowed on the affluent and rich in subtle, indirect, and loosely monitored ways. Moreover, many wealthfare programs overlap with each other and make complete separation and analysis difficult. Yet, even with these analytical problems, four basic types of wealthfare can tentatively be isolated: (1) government purchases in the economic market; (2) government price supports in this market; (3) government market regulation through export-import programs; and most important, (4) government tax expenditures. Wealthfare programs (1), (2), and (3) are conducted through the markets of America's complex economy, and we therefore group them together in our discussion. Program (4)—government tax expenditures—presents a more complex picture and is analyzed separately as the federal tax wealthfare system.

GOVERNMENT WEALTHFARE AND THE MARKET
Government Purchases in the Market
The federal government makes purchases in the market through the letting out of defense and civilian contracts. Such purchases are inevitable and necessary in a society where major productive and service organizations are privately (as opposed to state) owned. As critical and important as these contracts are in achieving national goals, they represent subsidies to the owners and workers of organizations holding contracts

with the government. And often the size of government purchases completely subverts free enterprise principles—especially when corporations such as Lockheed, Ling-Tempco-Vought, General Dynamics, and North American Rockwell do a majority of their business with the government. Other corporations—such as General Electric, Radio Corporation of America (RCA), Boeing, General Tire, Sperry-Rand, Westinghouse, Bendix, International Business Machines (IBM), Kaiser, General Telephone, Litton, and Pan American—sell such large quantities of goods and services to the government that their overall operations would be seriously threatened if the government suddenly took its business elsewhere.

Several features of these economic liaisons need to be emphasized. First, a disproportionate number of contracts go to large corporations controlling large sections of basic industries. As a result, economic stability increasingly depends on *continued* liaisons, even if government is dissatisfied or the corporation fails to meet its contract obligations. Second, large corporations tend to have clear and comprehensive contracts with blue-collar and white-collar workers, and as a result union workers' salaries are comparatively high. In addition, government often allows corporations to incur cost overruns and thus to avoid financial hardship and perhaps bankruptcy. Thirdly, the economic activity required by government contracts usually involves a considerable amount of brainpower, and so contracted corporations employ large proportions of professional and managerial personnel whose salaries are kept high by a continued flow of contract money.

Government contracts undoubtedly provide vital goods and services. But they subsidize only some sectors of the work force—the affluent blue-collar, white-collar, and professional workers. Further, corporations that do large amounts of government business can usually offer their owners (wealthy stockholders) substantial profits. Thus, government contracts are "make work" and "make profits" for the affluent and rich. When government contracts are compared with actual or proposed "make work" for the poor, rather noticeable differences in salary, fringe benefits, job security, and working conditions become evident. Government is rarely as generous in the purchase of the labor of the poor as it is in the purchase of the labor of the more affluent. The latter are organized by unions and professional associations and work for large corporations. These corporations are owned by the wealthy and are more and more the basis of the economic stability of the nation. Clearly, government contracts have a selective impact and can be considered a form of wealthfare.

Government Price Policies

Government regulates the price of many goods and commodities in the market, including many dairy and agricultural products. The actual subsidy mechanisms are complex, but they usually involve either (1) efforts to regulate the ratio of supply to demand in the open market or (2) efforts to directly control prices that can be charged for goods in the market. When supply and demand are regulated, manufacturers' productivity can be controlled (either encouraged or discouraged), or—as is more often true—exports or imports can be encouraged or discouraged in ways that affect supply and demand. When prices are regulated, the government artificially allows prices to be above or below what they would be if supply and demand forces in the market were allowed to determine price levels. But when prices are kept low, the government usually makes up the difference with a cash subsidy.

As with government contracts, price regulation is designed to affect large sectors of the economy and large organizations in them. Such regulation is undoubtedly required to control supplies and prices on many necessary goods, but regulation tends to benefit the unionized and well-paid white-collar workers as well as the owners of large corporations. Profits and wages are usually (not always, of course) maintained at high levels, and thus price regulation often represents a wealthfare subsidy to the more affluent and wealthy sectors of the economy.

Government Export-Import Policies

Export-import programs—quotas, taxes, credits, and so on—are intended to control the ratio of supply and demand of goods by limiting, encouraging, or taxing (to make goods comparable in price) the importation and exportation of goods. Further, at times government offers export or import monopolies to companies on a contract basis, thereby regulating both the flow of goods in the market and the profits of particular organizations in the market.

Export-import policies are usually designed to protect large companies and critical industries. When imports are limited, competition in the domestic market is discouraged, and the result is that prices, wages, and profits are kept higher than they would be otherwise. Similarly, by encouraging exports, the supply relative to demand is decreased, and again prices, wages, and profits are kept high. The populace, particularly the poor, feels this form of subsidy in higher prices. But the affluent make a net profit on the subsidy because their wages are kept high enough so that they can live with higher prices. Unfortunately the poor, who are least able to pay higher prices, do not receive compensatory benefits. And for the wealthy, who manage and own the affected corporations, profits are maintained. Thus, although some export-import programs are necessary in a world political economy, they often represent a wealthfare subsidy to the affluent and wealthy while forcing the poor to pay higher prices.

These three forms of market subsidy—government contracts, price programs, and export-import policies—are an important source of wealthfare. But they are probably less blatant and more necessary than the fourth major type of subsidy: federal tax expenditures. It is to an analysis of this form of wealthfare that the major portion of this chapter is dedicated. For in the end, it is tax wealthfare that is probably the most inequitable.

THE FEDERAL TAX WEALTHFARE SYSTEM

It has been estimated that present federal tax codes bestow between $65 and $77 billion per year to individuals and corporations—most of it to affluent and rich individuals and to large corporations and their owners.[1] At the state and local levels, data on how much money is passed on to the citizenry are scarce, but, as we shall see, the amounts are substantial.

It certainly does not take a social scientist to tell the average citizen that taxes cut drastically into spendable income. And yet, despite widespread discontent with high taxes, most Americans are only dimly aware of the degree to which tax laws promote inequality. Most taxes are regressive—that is, they take larger portions of the incomes of the less affluent than of the incomes of the wealthy. In addition, supposedly progressive taxes, which are intended to take a greater portion of the incomes of the affluent and the wealthy, in actuality tax the superrich, the affluent, and the poor at shockingly similar rates.[2] Tax laws thus represent an enormous wealthfare subsidy, and just how they promote vast inequality in America requires detailed examination.

The Legal Principles of Progressivity and Fairness

Taxes have probably been a source of discontent ever since governments began extracting them. As every student of American history knows, discontent with the taxing system of the English Crown—taxation without representation—was one of the causes of the American Revolution. In the effort to diminish the inevitable discontent associated with paying taxes, the principle of *progressivity* has become an important legal doctrine. Basically, this principle asserts that taxes should be assessed in accordance with ability to pay. Those individuals with little income should pay a smaller proportion of their income in taxes, while those with higher incomes should pay a progressively larger portion of their income in taxes as income rises. Progressivity in tax rates is not designed to level income to the point where everybody makes the same amount of money. Such a philosophy would violate basic American values of activism, achievement, and materialism, which stress the appropriateness of winners in competition enjoying their material success. The doctrine of progressivity only dictates that those with more income and assets should pay a larger portion of their wealth in taxes. They have more to give, and even after paying taxes they will have more left with which to realize the value of materialism.

Even without invoking the principle of progressivity, the *doctrine of fairness* of the Tenth Amendment, which first authorized Congress to collect income tax, argues that *all* dollars from whatever source must be subject to taxation. Unfortunately this doctrine is violated by the proliferation of tax loophole laws in federal and state income tax codes. These loopholes allow many dollars—usually those of the rich—to go untaxed, leading one cynic to observe that "some dollars are more equal than others."

Table 1 presents examples of how the principle of progressivity is violated by the structure of state income, local property, and federal social security taxes. Local property and state income taxes are supposed to be progressive, but as Table 1 reveals, they do not apply to *all* property or income of affluent groups. In fact, the more money and property individuals have, the less this money and property is subject to taxation. This situation violates the principle of fairness, because more of the dollars and assets of the poor are taxed than of the affluent. Thus, as is revealed by the decreasing percentages of taxed income as income rises in Table 1, it is clear that the lower-income groups pay a larger proportion of their income to state and local governments. A similar pattern is evident for federal social security taxes. Much of the income of the affluent is not subject to social security taxes, whereas an increasing proportion of the income of less affluent wage earners is—again, violating the *doctrine of fairness.*

Table 1 Percentages of Income Paid Out in Various Taxes for 1968

Total Family Income	Social Security Tax (percent)	State and Local Taxes		
		State (percent)	Property (percent)	Total (percent)
Under $2,000	7.6	6.6	16.2	27.2
$2,000–$4,000	6.5	4.9	7.5	15.7
$4,000–$6,000	6.7	4.1	4.8	12.1
$6,000–$8,000	6.8	3.6	3.8	10.7
$8,000–$10,000	6.2	3.3	3.6	10.1
$10,000–$15,000	5.8	2.9	3.6	9.9
$15,000–$25,000	4.6	2.4	3.6	9.4
$25,000–$50,000	2.5	1.8	2.7	7.8
Over $50,000	1.0	1.1	2.0	6.7

Source: Philip M. Stern, *The Rape of the Taxpayer* (New York: Random House, 1973), p. 24. Reprinted by permission of Harold Ober Associates Incorporated and Random House. Copyright © 1972, 1973 by Philip Stern.

State sales taxes, which apply the same rate to all taxpayers, also violate the principle of progressivity.[3] Thus, a clear pattern of inequity in tax laws is evident. Data on just how much of an impact these violations of the principles of progressivity and fairness have on inequality are not available. However, the impact of the federal income tax—the biggest tax of all—can be discerned from available data. Because the federal income tax is *on paper* highly progressive, the breakdown of this progressivity enables us to visualize how specific cultural and social forces operate to create tax inequality at the federal level.

In Table 2, the tax rate schedule for individual income is reproduced. As can be seen, the schedule is highly progressive. Those in very high income brackets are required to pay up to 70 percent of their income in federal taxes. Obviously, the federal income tax burden does not represent the full tax burden of Americans, because often they must also pay sales taxes, excise taxes, property taxes, state income taxes, and social security taxes. Although this tax burden is extensive, few Americans would give up the local, state, and federal services that are financed by these taxes. But, while a 70 percent income tax may seem excessively high, it should be remembered that those making this much money do so in an environment protected and regulated by government. Further, a 70 percent tax on a multimillion dollar income leaves a lot of money for enjoying the good things in life.

The federal income tax schedule on corporations does not need to be represented in a table, because the tax rate is essentially the same— 48 percent—on all corporate income. Thus, income tax on individuals is supposed to be highly progressive, while that on corporations is to be constant.

Table 2 Nominal Tax Rates, 1974, at Selected Levels of Taxable Income for Married Taxpayers Filing Joint Returns

Taxable Income	Nominal Rate (percent)
$ 1,000	14.0
$ 2,000	14.5
$ 3,000	15.0
$ 4,000	15.5
$ 8,000	17.3
$ 12,000	18.8
$ 16,000	20.4
$ 20,000	21.9
$ 24,000	23.6
$ 28,000	25.4
$ 32,000	27.1
$ 36,000	28.7
$ 40,000	30.4
$ 44,000	32.0
$ 52,000	34.7
$ 64,000	38.2
$ 76,000	40.8
$ 88,000	43.2
$100,000	45.2
$120,000	48.0
$140,000	50.3
$160,000	52.2
$180,000	54.0
$200,000	55.5
Over $200,000	55.5% of $200,000 + 70% of over $200,000

Source: Internal Revenue Service Form 1040, Schedule Y, p. 20, 1974. Rates are calculated at the upper limit of taxable income intervals listed on Form 1040 (except, of course, for the highest interval).

These taxes on income are to be levied on *net* income; that is, they are to be assessed only after the expenses incurred in generating the income are deducted from gross income. These deductions from gross income are usually termed *structural aspects* of a tax schedule, because they are directly connected to assessing taxes on net income. It would indeed be unfair to tax only gross income without allowing individuals to subtract their direct costs and expenses in making this income. After all, it costs more to make money in some activities than in others; and hence, it is appropriate that only net income be taxed.

Just what constitutes a legitimate expense, however, has not been easy to determine. Over the years, under pressure from high income individuals and corporations, the number of legitimate expenditures has increased, allowing larger and larger deductions from gross income and reducing the next taxable income. Additionally, pressures from powerful individuals and corporations and the desire of government to encourage specific activities have created an expanding body of laws. These have been incorporated into the tax codes and allow further reductions in taxable net income. The exact nature of the tax benefit varies, but common loopholes include exclusions from income, credits against taxes, preferential tax rates, deferrals of tax, accelerated depreciations, and depletion allowances.

These loopholes in the tax structure are increasingly being viewed as *tax expenditures*, because they represent government subsidies to individuals and corporations. These loopholes have little relation to the costs incurred in deriving income and are not a part of the basic tax structure. The revenues lost to the government through these loopholes represent an expenditure that utilizes the tax system as a means for distributing money. As such, the lost revenues represent expenditures from a *tax budget*. These expenditures could be made directly out of the regular government budget; but if this were done, the inequity of these tax wealthfare payments would be more visible and would provoke indignation in the general population.

Types of Tax Loopholes

To appreciate just how these expenditures in a tax budget occur, it is necessary to examine briefly the basic types of legal mechanisms used by individuals and corporations to escape the provisions of the basic tax structure. There are five general types of laws used in tax expenditure budgets:[4] (1) *exclusions* from gross income, (2) *deductions* from gross income, (3) *tax credits*, (4) *special tax rates*, and (5) *tax sheltering*. It is through these legal loopholes that wealthfare payments to the rich and affluent are made.

Exclusions and Exemptions from Income. The federal tax codes allow individuals and corporations to exclude particular types of income. As far as the tax laws are concerned, this income does not count as part of an individual's or corporation's gross income and thus it escapes taxes—a provision that makes "some dollars more equal than others." For wage earners receiving a salary, there are many exclusions, including the income in kind coming from an expense account, sick pay, exercise of stock options, income earned abroad, employers' contributions to medical insurance, social security, and retirement.[5] Such exclusions keep wage earners in lower tax brackets, while allowing them to enjoy the benefits of extra, untaxed monies.

Individuals who receive some forms of income transfer payments are allowed to exclude that income from the tax collector. Social security, welfare, and unemployment benefits are conspicuous examples. Individuals and corporations as investors are allowed enormous exclusions—for example, the first $100 on stock dividends,[6] the interest on life insurance savings, the interest on state and local bonds,[7] and some forms of capital gains.[8]

The total impact of these various exclusions accounts for nearly one-third of the total tax expenditure budget. Some dollars are not taxed, and as will be even more evident in our subsequent presentation of a detailed tax expenditure budget (see also footnotes 6 and 7), the majority of these expenditures are for individuals in the upper-income fifth. Exclusions from income laws thus represent a massive wealthfare program for the rich and affluent.

Deductions from Gross Income. Under current law, certain deductions from gross income are allowed, thereby reducing taxable income even further. Some of these deductions are a necessary part of the tax structure, because they allow individuals and corporations to be taxed on only their net income—gross income less the costs incurred in amassing this income. However, the proliferation of laws expanding the number of deductions has obscured this structural relation between income and costs. Deductions from income have come to bear little relationship to actual costs incurred. This situation underscores how a necessary structural feature of any tax system can be transformed into a massive tax expenditure by the federal government.[9]

For individual consumers, certain costs incurred in living are deductible from the top of gross income, thereby reducing the tax bracket and hence the rate of taxation. The deduction of interest, medical expenses, or moving costs related to changes in work represent typical deductions (which come on top of personal exemptions or exclusions for each member of a family). For individuals who assume the role of investor, however, deductions become a means for protecting or sheltering all gross income. For example, 50 percent of income from capital gains can be deducted,[10] and the remaining 50 percent is then taxed at a rate which is one-half of the rate applicable to earned income.[11]

Or, to take another example, investments in various economic activities can be depreciated in a short period of time rather than over the actual life of the investment. Investors do not have to wait for real estate, oil, cattle, orchards, and other investments to wear out. They can deduct the depreciation within just a brief period after purchase, thereby cutting the cost of the item and perhaps sheltering income from other sources by showing a tax loss. If depreciation was a structural aspect of the tax system, then only a small amount of depreciation would be deducted each year over the *entire* life of the investment. And further, depreciation on appreciating investments, such as real estate and cattle, would not be allowed. The fact that the deductions from these and many other types of investments no longer bear a relation to the costs involved in deriving income from the investments underscores the extent to which they represent tax expenditures. For corporations, the accelerated depreciation of equipment represents an even greater tax expenditure than that for individuals. Other investments, such as pollution control, coal mining safety equipment, employer child care, and on-the-job training, are also given special tax treatment through short-term amortization and then deduction from gross income.[12]

Similarly, oil and mineral extracting companies can, in addition to their depletion allowances (which are exemptions from gross income), enjoy the benefits of accelerating their depletion of resources for tax purposes. Thus, oil companies can claim, for tax purposes, a large proportion of depletion of resources in the first few years of a new well, when in fact the oil well may not be fully depleted for many years to come. This hefty deduction of mythical depletion allows oil companies and other extractive industries to reduce on paper their gross income and thus to protect profits from taxation—a tax wealthfare system that costs billions of dollars per year.

For both individuals and corporations in business, just what constitutes an expense incurred in the process of running the business no longer has much relation to actual costs involved in making an income from the business. For example, expense accounts, the elaborate entertaining of potential clients, the extensive and often unnecessary travel by executives, and other similar practices far exceed what is actually necessary to run a business. But these can all be deducted from gross income—and so, in effect, the government is buying theater and airline tickets for executives and entertaining them in elegant hotels and restaurants.

In sum, then, tax laws on deductions from gross income have become expenditures in a tax budget. Although it is not easy to define exactly what constitutes a legitimate cost, it is clear that deductions from income bear little relationship to costs. And each year these loopholes represent a multibillion dollar subsidy, or wealthfare payment, to the rich and affluent.

Tax Credits. Another form of tax expenditure is the credit against taxes. With tax credits, an individual or corporation receives a percent of credit against taxes for certain kinds of activities and income. For example, the elderly receive a credit against taxes of 15 percent of their retirement income up to $1,524 for a single person and $2,286 for a married couple. Corporations that invest in machinery receive credit against taxes of 7 percent of the cost of the machinery.[13] Tax credits are less frequent than other forms of governmental tax expenditure for two reasons: (1) the rate of credit remains constant and does not rise with tax brackets—and so it is a less appealing form of wealthfare; and (2) the credit is a highly visible subsidy and is not as easily hidden in technical tax language as are exclusions and deductions—and so it is a risky form of subsidy.

Special Tax Rates. Under the law some types of income are taxed at lower rates than others. The most costly tax expenditure of all—capital gains—is the best example of a special tax rate. For individual capital gains—that is, the profit from selling some asset such as real estate, stocks, or equipment—one-half of the gain is automatically excluded from taxation (although the technical wording of the law calls this exclusion a deduction). Then, the remaining half can be taxed at a maximum rate of 25 percent for the first $50,000 and at a maximum rate of 35 percent over $50,000. Even if an individual makes $10,000,000 in a year from other sources, 25 percent for $50,000 of capital gains income and 35 percent for any capital gains over this amount are the maximum rates for capital gains income. Corporations similarly get special tax treatment for their capital gains, although the precise rates vary in a more complex pattern.

Capital gains laws are significant because they represent a special rate for the wealthy, much of whose income comes from capital gains. In Table 3, the percent of the population in various income groups in 1969 who receive capital gains income are listed in one column.[14] In the adjacent column, the percent of their total income derived from capital gains is listed. As is obvious, it is the rich who make use of the capital gains tax rate, since 82 percent of their income is in the form of capital gains. The rich thus have their own tax rate.

Table 3 Capital Gains Income for Different Income Levels

Selected Income Groups	Individuals Who Have Capital Gains Income (percent of population)	Income From Capital Gains (percent of income)
Under $5,000	4.5	1.9
$10,000–$25,000	14.0	2.4
$50,000–$100,000	55.3	15.6
Over $1,000,000	90.9	82.1

Source: Philip M. Stern, *The Rape of the Taxpayer* (New York: Random House, 1973), p. 96. Reprinted by permission of Harold Ober Associates Incorporated and Random House. Copyright © 1972, 1973 by Philip Stern.

In Table 4, the cumulative percentages of the total capital gains income received by diverse income groups are summarized.[15] The rich, who comprise only 3 percent of all taxpayers, take in nearly 65 percent of the total capital gains income.

Table 4 Cumulative Percentages of Total Capital Gains Income Received by Selected Income Groups

Income Groups	Their Percentage of Total Capital Gains Income
$200,000 and over	27.8
$100,000 and over	37.7
$ 50,000 and over	49.9
$ 25,000 and over	64.5
$ 10,000 and over	87.1

Source: Philip M. Stern, *The Rape of the Taxpayer* (New York: Random House, 1973), p. 95. Reprinted by permission of Harold Ober Associates Incorporated and Random House. Copyright © 1972, 1973 by Philip Stern.

In Table 5, the average tax wealthfare payments from the capital gains loophole to families of different income groups are summarized.[16] It is evident, then, that this special tax rate represents a massive wealthfare expenditure, an expenditure that perpetuates inequality in America.

Table 5 Average Wealthfare Payments from Capital Gains for Selected Income Groups

Income Level	Capital Gains Wealthfare Payment
$3,000–$5,000	$1
$5,000–$10,000	$8
$15,000–$20,000	$55
$20,000–$25,000	$120
$100,000–$500,000	$23,000
$500,000–$1,000,000	$165,000
Over $1,000,000	$641,000

Source: Philip M. Stern, *The Rape of the Taxpayer* (New York: Random House, 1973), p. 94. Reprinted by permission of Harold Ober Associates Incorporated and Random House. Copyright © 1972, 1973 by Philip Stern.

Tax Sheltering. Various combinations of current tax laws allow exemptions, deductions, credits, and special rates that produce another form of tax expenditure: the deferral of taxes through the creation of tax shelters. There is no explicit tax shelter law, but the collective impact of other laws creates an informal law that bestows billions of dollars on the wealthy each year.

The basics of tax sheltering involve a series of interrelated uses of the formal laws. (1) Accelerated depreciation and depletion, plus investment credits, allow investors in some industries and economic activities to show a paper loss on their investments, because the costs of such investments are bunched together in the first years of investments. Under more structural tax accounting procedures, depreciation would be spread out over the life of the investment, depletion would correspond to the actual depletion of resources, and credits for investments would not be allowed. (2) These paper losses are then deducted from gross income earned in the favored investment and—more importantly—in any other area. Thus, by showing a sufficiently large paper loss in one area of investment, income from other sources can be protected or sheltered by the large deduction allowed by the paper loss. (3) Laws allowing what is termed a *limited partnership* enable those with money to join up with those in favored industries—cattle, farming, oil, mining, orchards, ranching, real estate—without incurring *any* liabilities beyond the amount actually invested. Thus, the investor can lose only the money invested, protecting other assets if the investment fails. (4) Eventually, when the investment is sold and liquidated, it is taxed as capital gains—not as regular income—and thus receives the special rate of taxation accorded capital gains.

There are a number of massive federal subsidies to the rich in high income brackets built into sheltering procedures. First, the affluent have been able to avoid paying taxes on much income earned in areas totally unrelated to their investment in favored economic activity. The large deduction from the paper loss allows them to lower their tax bracket and thus pay less tax (and sometimes, virtually no tax) on large amounts of gross income. Second, the large depletion on the investment creates a situation where taxes on profits from the investment are deferred until the investment is liquidated. This deferral of taxes represents an interest-free loan from the government to the investor. Third, smart investors borrow all the money they invest in favored activities, thereby deriving all the benefits of a tax shelter, while adding another deduction: the interest on the borrowed money. In reality, the government pays the interest by allowing the investor to deduct it directly from other income while not paying taxes on the profits of the favored investment. Fourth, when taxes come due with liquidation, one-half of the profit is excluded (technically, deducted) and the other half is taxed at 25 percent (for under $50,000 profit) or at 35 percent (for over $50,000 profit).

Only taxpayers who have money to invest and are in high income brackets can take advantage of tax shelters. The large deduction allowed from the paper loss then allows taxpayers to lower their tax bracket and pay less tax. And when deferred taxes finally come due, the rich have their own special tax rate—the capital gains rate. The laws that allow this activity are written for the wealthy. Average wage earners rarely have much extra money to invest, and even if they make a small investment, their tax bracket is not high enough to enable them to take full advantage of the paper loss. Thus, tax shelters are wealthfare for the rich.

The types of laws that guide tax expenditures represent a subsidy to the affluent and rich. As such, they violate the principles of progressivity and fairness. We will analyze the beliefs that justify this wealthfare, but first we consider some of the consequences of these laws on the federal government's budgetary practices.

The Tax Expenditure Budget

Whether or not tax loopholes are considered necessary incentives for key investments and industries, it is clear that they represent government expenditures on some segments of the society. Because these expenditures are embedded in the tax codes, they assume a complexity that often hides the beneficiaries of government aid. Welfare to the poor is a direct expenditure item in governmental budgets, because public sentiment requires that such expenditures be carefully monitored. But in contrast, when expenditures for the wealthy are enmeshed in the structural provisions of the tax code, an accurate record is more difficult to attain and the privileged are subjected to less scrutiny.

Tax expenditures are grafted onto the basic tax structure as a means of giving subsidies to the affluent and favored industries. Only recently has the expenditure nature of these subsidies been acknowledged by the Treasury Department and by congressional committees. As awareness of the magnitude of government expenditures through the tax system has increased, attempts at constructing a tax expenditure budget have been made. This budget is intended to supplement the regular direct expenditure budget and to give an indication of the areas in which the government is spending uncollected tax revenues. In Table 6, the tax

Table 6 Federal Income Tax Expenditures Calendar Year 1972 (by budget function)

	Corpora-tions	Indi-viduals	Total
		(millions of dollars)	
National Defense			
Exclusion of benefits and allowances to armed forces personnel		700	700
International Affairs and Finance			
Exemption for certain income earned abroad by United States citizens		50	50
Western Hemisphere Trade Corporations	50		50
Exclusion of gross-up on dividends of less-developed-country corporations	60		60
Deferral of income of controlled foreign corporations	300	25	325
Exclusion of income earned in United States possessions	80	10	90
Deferral of export income (DISC)	240	—	240
Total:	730	85	815
Agriculture			
Farming: expensing and capital gain treatment	50	850	900
Timber: capital gain treatment for certain income	125	50	175
Total:	175	900	1,075

Table 6 (Continued)

	Corpora-tions	Indi-viduals	Total
		(millions of dollars)	
Natural Resources			
Expensing of exploration and development costs	580	70	650
Excess of percentage over cost depletion	1,400	300	1,700
Capital gain treatment of royalties on coal and iron ore	5	—	5
Total:	1,985	370	2,355
Commerce and Transportation			
Investment credit	3,050	750	3,800
Depreciation on buildings (other than rental housing) in excess of straight-line depreciation	330	170	500
Asset depreciation range system for depreciation	2,100	200	2,300
Dividend exclusion		300	300
Capital gains: corporation (other than farming and timber)	400		400
Capital gains: individuals (other than farming and timber)		9,000	9,000
Bad debt reserves of financial institutions	400		400
Exemption of credit unions	90		90
Deductibility of interest on consumer credit		1,100	1,100
Expensing of research and development expenditures	570		570
$25,000 corporate surtax exemption	2,500		2,500
Deferral of tax on shipping companies	30		30
Five-year amortization of railroad rolling stock	80	—	80
Total:	9,550	11,520	21,070
Housing and Community Development			
Deductibility of interest on mortgages on owner-occupied homes		3,500	3,500
Deductibility of property taxes on owner-occupied homes		3,250	3,250
Depreciation on rental housing in excess of straight-line depreciation	350	250	600
Five-year amortization of housing rehabilitation expenditures	65	100	165
Deferral of capital gain on sale to occupants of certain low-income housing	—	—	n.a.
Total:	415	7,100	7,515

Table 6 (Continued)

	Corpora-tions	Indi-viduals	Total
		(millions of dollars)	

Health, Labor and Welfare

	Corpora-tions	Indi-viduals	Total
Exclusion of employer-provided disability insurance benefits		175	175
Provisions relating to aged: combined cost for additional exemptions, retirement income credit, and exclusion of social security payments		3,550	3,550
Additional exemption for blind		10	10
Exclusion of unemployment insurance benefits		700	700
Sick pay exclusion		225	225
Exclusion of workmen's compensation benefits		375	375
Exclusion of public assistance benefits		65	65
Net exclusion of pension contributions and earnings:			
Plans for employees		4,000	4,000
Plans for self-employed persons		200	200
Exclusion of other employee benefits:			
Premiums on group term life insurance		550	550
Accident and accidental death premiums		35	35
Medical insurance premiums and medical care		2,500	2,500
Privately financed supplementary unemployment benefits		5	5
Meals and lodging		170	170
Exclusion of interest on life insurance savings		1,200	1,200
Deductibility of charitable contributions (other than education)		3,100	3,100
Deductibility of medical expenses		1,900	1,900
Deductibility of child and dependent care and household expenses		180	180
Deductibility of casualty losses		150	150
Standard deduction in excess of minimum standard deduction		1,040	1,040
Five-year amortization of pollution control facilities (pre-1969 plants)	25		25
Credit for employment of public assistance recipients under WIN program	20		20
Five-year amortization of employer child care and on-the-job training facilities	10	——	10
Total:	55	20,130	20,185

Table 6 (Continued)

	Corpora-tions	Indi-viduals	Total
		(millions of dollars)	
Education			
Additional parental personal exemption for students		640	640
Deductibility of contributions to educational institutions		275	275
Exclusion of scholarships and fellowships	____	125	125
Total:		1,040	1,040
Veterans Benefits and Services			
Exclusion of certain veterans benefits		480	480
General Government			
Credit and deduction for political contributions		100	100
Aid to State and Local Financing			
Exemption of interest on state and local debt	1,900	1,000	2,900
Deductibility of nonbusiness state and local taxes (other than on owner-occupied homes)	____	5,300	5,300
Total:	1,900	6,300	8,200

Source: From "Estimates of Federal Tax Expenditures," House Committee on Ways and Means, June 1, 1973. In Stanley S. Surrey, *Pathways to Tax Reform* (Cambridge, Mass.: Harvard University Press, 1973), pp. 8–12.

expenditure budget for 1972 is summarized. These expenditures represent over one-quarter of the total direct expenditure budget for that year, revealing that the direct expenditure budget underestimates government expenses. We cannot summarize the exact contents of each law and the exact mechanism by which each operates. But a cursory glance down the expenditure items shows that the laws discussed earlier —under the general categories of exclusions, deductions, credits, special rates, and avoidance and deferrals through shelters—embrace all of the expenditure items.

One way to visualize this long list of expenditures is to compare the amounts and types of expenditures on individuals and corporations. It is convenient to view the tax expenditures for individuals as (1) consumers, (2) investors, (3) noninvestment income earners, and (4) recipients of income transfer payments.[17]

Consumers. Around twenty-one billion dollars is spent by the government through the tax budget on individual consumers. The breakdown of these expenditures reveals the following profile:[18]

Standard deduction	1.0 billion
allowed as alternative to itemization of personal deductions	
Support of philanthropy	3.5 billion
charity deductions	
gifts to education	
gifts to election process	
Home ownership	6.8 billion
interest deductions	
property tax deductions	
Governmental taxes	5.3 billion
nonbusiness state and local taxes (excluding property tax)	
Medical services	1.9 billion
deductions for treatment and medicines	
Credit purchases	1.1 billion
deduction of interest	
Education	705.0 million
exclusions of scholarships and fellowships	
additional exemptions for students	
Casualty losses	150.0 million
deductions for losses	
Home services	180.0 million
child care and household expense deductions	
Total	20.7 billion

Investors.[19] Individuals who invest in the economy and government projects represent the second largest individual beneficiaries of tax expenditures. This group realizes around $13 billion[20] per year in government subsidy, which breaks down as follows:

General Investment	12 billion
exclusions on stock dividends	
capital gains treatment in general	
exclusions of interest on state and local bonds	
exclusions of interest on life insurance	
real estate capital gains treatment	
Shelter investments	1 billion
Total	13 billion

Noninvestment Income Earners.[21] In this segment of tax expenditure, beneficiaries are wage and salary earners as well as those deriving various forms of professional income. Most of the expenditures for these individuals come from the various types of fringe benefits associated with different occupations.

Wage and salary employees
    fringe benefits provided by employers
    exclusions of pension plans
    insurance exclusions
    expense accounts
    unemployment and sick leave benefits
Government programs
    unemployment insurance and
        workman's compensation exclusions
    exclusions of benefits to armed forces personnel
Executive compensation
    exclusions of income earned abroad
    stock option treatment

Total	9.4 billion

Recipients of Income Transfer Payments.[22] The government uses the tax system to provide income for individuals who are in need or who have served the government in various ways. These income transfer payments—welfare administered through the tax system—amount to around 4 billion a year tax expenditures:

Welfare benefits	3.6 billion
provisions for elderly	
exclusion of welfare assistance	
exemptions for the blind	
Veterans benefits	480.0 million
Total	4.0 billion

Corporations and specific industries receive billions of dollars each year through the tax expenditure system. The tax benefits given to corporations through the tax expenditure budget have been increasing in recent years, as is revealed by the fact that corporate taxation came to 4.3 percent of the total GNP in 1963 and only 3.7 percent in 1973.[23] Because corporate taxes are not progressive—they remain on paper at a constant 48 percent—they should remain a constant proportion of the total GNP. A drop in this proportion reveals growing tax expenditures for corporations by the federal government. These expenditures can be broken down into two general categories: (1) expenditures for all corporations; and (2) special industry expenditures.

Expenditures for all corporations
    investment credits for machinery and
        equipment purchases
    deductions of excess depreciation
    deductions of special research and development
        expenditures

capital gains treatment: 30 percent rate
deductions of excess depreciation on buildings
amortization over five years of certain expenses

	Total	8.3 billion

Special industry expenditures
  natural resource industries
    depletion allowances
    expenses of exploration and development costs
    amortization of mine safety equipment
  financial organizations
    exemption of interest on bonds
    deduction of bad debts
    exemptions of credit unions
  lumber industry
    capital gains treatment
  international corporations
    exclusion of income from foreign subsidies
    exclusion for specific activities in underdeveloped countries
    exclusion of income earned in United States possessions
    deferral of export income
  shipping
    deferral of tax on shipping companies
  farming
    favored expense and capital gains treatment
  real estate
    deductions of excess depreciation
    amortization treatment
  railroads
    amortization treatment on cars and engines

	Total	6.7 billion

Who Benefits from Tax Expenditures?

We have argued repeatedly that tax expenditures promote inequality
in America by subsidizing the privilege of the affluent and rich. The
mathematics of a progressive tax system which has moved from a structural to expenditure profile documents this assertion. The progressivity
of the tax structure assures, in strictly mathematical terms, that the higher
an individual's tax rate, the greater will be the benefits from tax expenditures. For example, a deduction of $1,000 is worth $250 to someone
in a 25 percent tax bracket and $500 to another taxpayer in a 50 percent
bracket. Thus, tax loopholes are worth less to low income taxpayers—
making the subsidies wealthfare. But the mathematical story does not
end here, because large deductions (or exemptions, credits, and so on)
will lower an individual's tax bracket, and thus the tax rate. Because
tax depends upon *reported net* income, exemptions, deductions, deferrals and other tax loopholes lower the amount of income that is reported

and hence the tax that must be paid. The end result is that tax laws give the largest write-offs to the rich, and these write-offs then allow for reductions in the amount of taxable income. The mathematical inevitability of this process underscores the inappropriateness of undermining the structural features of a progressive income tax with tax expenditures.

Coupled with the fact that tax laws contain loopholes available only to the affluent (not many poor can own stock, invest in machinery, form a corporation, and so on), the substance and mathematics of the tax system inevitably promote inequality. One way to visualize the extent to which these loopholes work for the rich is to pose the hypothetical question: Whose taxes would go up if tax expenditures were removed from the law? Table 7 summarizes the percentage increase in taxes that would result from closing the most conspicuous loopholes for individuals. We have excluded old age benefits from the analysis, because they represent special problems in analyzing the effects of tax expenditures on low-income groups. As can be seen from Table 7, the large increases in taxes would come from the very rich who make over $500,000 per year. Further, significant increases would occur for the affluent earning over $25,000. The important point is that the closing of the loopholes would restore progressivity in the tax structure, as is revealed by the virtual doubling of the taxes of the wealthy.

Table 7 Percentage Increase in Taxes for Selected Income Groups with Closing of Tax Loopholes

Income Group	Increase in Taxes (percent)
Under $3,000	18
$3,000–$5,000	16
$5,000–$10,000	17
$10,000–$15,000	22
$15,000–$20,000	23
$20,000–$25,000	24
$25,000–$50,000	28
$50,000–$100,000	45
$100,000–$500,000	73
$500,000–$1,000,000	98
Over $1,000,000	96

Source: Stanley S. Survey, *Pathways to Tax Reform* (Cambridge, Mass.: Harvard University Press, 1973), p. 69. Copyright © 1973 by Harvard University Press.

Looking at the issue of inequality in another way, Table 8 presents data giving a rough indication of the average *wealth*fare payment in 1972 to various income groupings through these loopholes. The figures in the far right-hand column represent the difference between tax liabilities under the current law and what they would be if the loopholes were closed. This difference represents the average amount of tax that individuals under present law can avoid. This difference is the wealthfare payment from the federal government each year.

Table 8 Average Yearly Wealthfare Payment in 1972 for Selected Income Groups

Income Group	Average Payment
Under $3,000	$15.00
$3,000–$5,000	$143.00
$5,000–$10,000	$286.00
$10,000–$15,000	$411.00
$15,000–$20,000	$600.00
$20,000–$25,000	$871.00
$25,000–$50,000	$1,729.00
$50,000–$100,000	$5,896.00
$100,000–$500,000	$29,503.00
$500,000–$1,000,000	$216,751.00
Over $1,000,000	$726,198.00

Source: Stanley S. Surrey. *Pathways to Tax Reform* (Cambridge, Mass.: Harvard University Press, 1973), p. 71. Copyright © 1973 by Harvard University Press.

In sum, then, it is clear that the tax expenditure budget represents federal subsidies to the rich and affluent through the tax structure. In allowing these subsidies, the federal government undermines the principle of progressivity in the income tax. Table 9 summarizes the progressive erosion of progressivity through use of tax loopholes. As can be seen in the "Structural Tax Rate" column, the structural codes of the tax law reveal a high degree of progressivity, with over a 40 percent difference between the tax rates of the average worker in the $10,000 to $11,000 income bracket and that of the superwealthy earning over a million. With the help of the loopholes, however, this difference in rates has been reduced to 25 percent, as can be seen by comparing the structural tax rate figures with taxes actually paid. In the far right column, the percentages saved by application of loopholes are summarized. Notice the high degree of progressivity in the savings, revealing again how much the loopholes benefit the affluent and rich.

Table 9 Structural and Actual Tax Rates and Percentage Savings in Taxes for Selected Income Groups

Income Groups	Structural Tax Rate (percent)	Taxes Actually Paid (percent)	Savings from Loophole (percent)
$2,000–$3,000	1.9	0.5	1.4
$3,000–$6,000	7.5	2.8	4.7
$10,000–$11,000	12.4	7.6	4.8
$20,000–$25,000	20.8	12.1	8.7
$75,000–$100,000	46.0	26.8	19.2
$200,000–$500,000	58.0	29.6	28.4
$900,000–$1,000,000	60.5	30.4	30.1
Over $1,000,000	63.1	32.1	31.0

Source: Philip M. Stern, *The Rape of the Taxpayer* (New York: Random House, 1972), p. 11. Reprinted by permission of Harold Ober Associates Incorporated and Random House. Copyright © 1972, 1973 by Philip Stern.

Turning to corporate taxation, the erosion of the statutory rates by loopholes is evident. Corporate taxes are supposed to be assessed at a constant 48 percent rate on profits, but the general loopholes available to all corporations, plus the additional subsidies to special industries, significantly reduce this tax rate. In Table 10,[24] the statutory tax rate of 48 percent is compared to the effective rate (after the use of loopholes) for 1965 and 1972. Further, the table attempts to indicate just which tax expenditures provide the most subsidy. As can be seen at the bottom of the table, corporations have consistently reduced their taxes by over 10 percent, but equally interesting, they are doing better at tax reduction in 1972 than in 1965. The fact is particularly significant because in 1969 a Tax Reform Act was passed.[25] Apparently, this act had little impact on corporations. (We will examine this 1969 act shortly.)

From this review of the individual and corporate beneficiaries of tax expenditures, it is clear that wealthy individuals and corporations in oil, finance, and other favored industries get the lion's share of wealthfare

Table 10 Factors Reducing Tax Rates for Corporations in 1965 and 1972

		1965 (percent)		1972 (percent)
Statutory Rate		48.0		48.0
Less surtax exemption	2.5		2.2	
investment credit	2.4		3.0	
excess depreciation on machinery and equipment				
ADR class life system	___		1.4	
Reduction due to general tax expenditures	4.9		6.6	
General effective rate		43.1		41.4
Less exclusion of state and local bond interest	.9		1.8	
excess percentage depletion	2.2		1.8	
capital gains rate	.8		.6	
excess exploration and development costs	.4		.4	
excess bad debt reserves	.6		.4	
excess depreciation on buildings	.5		.4	
Western Hemisphere Trade Corporation rate	.2		.2	
DISC	___		.1	
Reduction due to specialized tax expenditures	5.6		5.7	
Overall effective rate, including specially benefited industries		37.5		35.7

Source: Stanley S. Surrey, *Pathways to Tax Reform* (Cambridge, Mass.: Harvard University Press, 1973), p. 77. Copyright © 1973 by Harvard University Press.

payments. By conservative estimates these payments amount to at least $65 billion a year in subsidy. When this figure is contrasted with the approximately $12 billion in transfer payments to the poor from the direct expenditure budget, it is obvious that tax expenditures are not counterbalanced by direct expenditures. The result is that tax laws in America perpetuate inequality.[26]

MAINTAINING THE WEALTHFARE STATE

The issue of government "doles" to citizens is a volatile one in American society. Basic values dictate the inappropriateness of government hand-outs in a society where achievements are supposed to come through the expenditure of individual effort in a free and open competitive arena. As we show in our analysis of welfare in the next chapter, these values have been translated into negative stereotypes about the poor. In light of this, it is curious that *wealth*fare recipients escape extreme stereo-typing, especially if it is recognized that wealthfare costs more than welfare. Thus, critical questions requiring an answer include: How do wealthfare recipients avoid negative stereotyping? And if the rich were stereotyped as the poor are, would not public pressure force closure of tax loopholes?

The answers to these questions should give us a rough understanding of how wealthfare recipients are able to maintain their privilege. Howard Tuchman[27] has suggestively called the efforts by the affluent and rich to preserve their privilege a "war for wealth." And the warriors, in the words of Philip Stern, [28] are endowed "with all the energy and zeal that the threat of losing . . . hundreds of millions of dollars can provide." We should be cautious of the images invoked by the concept *war*, but since the poor have had a war on poverty waged on their behalf, we may find some insights in Tuchman's image.

In the war for wealth, a number of tactics and strategies are vigorously employed: (1) diversionary tactics, (2) guerilla maneuvers, and (3) delay-ing strategies. Frontal attacks in this war are usually avoided, because they might expose the degree to which basic values and beliefs are violated by the wealthy. The war for wealth is thus a quiet war, often fought behind closed congressional doors. The spoils that go to the victors in this combat are high: the tax dollars siphoned from the Treasury. Such tax pillage keeps taxes for most Americans too high, while depriving them of the benefits that well-financed government programs in the direct expenditure budget could provide. Thus, if we are to understand how the wealthfare state is maintained, it is necessary to examine the tactics and strategies used in the war for wealth.

Diversionary Tactics

The use of the tax codes for wealthfare subsidies is a diversionary tactic. When the structural features of tax laws are amended, subsidies appear more legitimate. A deduction or exemption from taxes is granted on the often incorrect assumption that some taxes are to be paid. The complexity of tax laws facilitates the concealment of the exact extent of subsidies. It is critical for wealthfare recipients that their government handouts be kept out of the direct expenditure budget. If tax expenditure items were stripped of respectability and complexity and placed in the direct expenditure budget, most of the subsidies would not be allowed. For example, in comparing a tax expenditure item such as interest deductions for home mortgages used by all home-owning Americans, inequality and inequity of subsidy would be exposed:[29]

Federal Home Ownership Subsidies
For a married couple with:

$200,000 income	*$10,000 income*	*No taxable income*
The government will pay $70 to the bank for each $100 of mortgage interest on the couple's home. The couple must pay $30.	The government will pay $19 to the bank for each $100 of mortgage interest on the couple's home. The couple must pay $81.	The government will pay nothing. The couple must pay all of the interest.

Or, to translate other tax expenditures into direct expenditure language:[30] the treasury department will pay $1.00 to a top bracket taxpayer who buys a tax exempt bond in order to provide 58¢ in assistance to local governments—a healthy commission for the taxpayer. Such subsidies, written into the tax laws, are deceptive. For example, current tax laws allow for medical deductions that exceed 3 percent of total income. But suppose a congressman wishes to introduce a "minor" tax change to give the elderly a break by allowing them to deduct all medical expenses. This sounds like a noble proposal because, as we all know, the elderly on fixed incomes deserve some help. But such "help" through the tax system is deceptive. The proposal would cost $200 million; of that, $90 million would go to persons with an annual income of over $40,000 and only $8 million would go to persons with incomes of less than $4,000.[31] Thus, tax relief is a diversionary tactic for achieving wealthfare.

These examples are sufficient to demonstrate that it is better to use the mechanism of direct expenditures to achieve tax relief or to subsidize particular types of activities. Direct expenditures give less money to the wealthy and facilitate a careful accounting of where the money is going. Perhaps one of the results of converting tax expenditures to direct expenditures would be to expose the extent to which they violate basic values, such as activism, achievement, freedom, and individualism. Thus, any such conversion would be discontinued or cut back (as welfare has been). It is for this reason, of course, that the wealthy want wealthfare payments diverted through the tax system. But more fundamentally, direct government subsidy of individuals by the government will be resisted, even when this procedure is preferable to indirect subsidy through the tax codes.

Indirect subsidy helps perpetuate inequality. Ironically, efforts to change this situation are likely to be resisted not only by the rich, who derive enormous benefits, but also by middle-income individuals who derive only small benefits. For example, if the government were to disallow the deduction of home mortgage interest payments from gross income, there would be resistance by middle-income groups whose benefits from this law are meager compared to those derived by the rich. In fact, middle-income groups must pay higher taxes than necessary to make these and other wealthfare payments to the rich. Blue-collar and white-collar individuals intensely resent taxation for welfare; and yet they would resist the changes in tax laws that would lower the wealthfare burden. Such is the nature of another diversionary tactic: give a little to the affluent majority in tax expenditures so that they will resist changes in the laws that bestow vast privilege on the rich. In this way, the rich enlist the cooperation of middle-income groups in an alliance that merely preserves privilege and inequality.

Guerilla Maneuvers

Tax loopholes are tacked onto the structural features of a progressive tax system in a piecemeal fashion. Rarely is a frontal assault undertaken, lest the self-interest of the wealthy be exposed. Rather, the progressivity of the tax structure is eroded by a persistent series of skirmishes. Tax reform laws are sometimes enacted, setting back some of the gains made in previous skirmishes, but the net result of selected political pressure on lawmakers is to expand tax expenditures.

One guerilla strategy is to take a special privilege loophole that is considered unfair and expose its unfairness; but rather than argue for closure of the loophole to restore equity, argue that the loophole should be extended to others in the name of fairness.[32] The use of one loophole to justify expansion of all loopholes is an effective tactic. This is evident, for example, from the granting of successive depletion allowances to coal, oil, and other extractive industries, including bricks, clay, gravel, mollusk shells, sand, and slate. One commentator has speculated that even users of supposedly inexhaustible resources, such as air and water, may be given depletion allowances. A company "extracting" the steam from geysers to drive electric generators recently suggested such an allowance.[33]

Probably the best example of the effect of piecemeal political pressure on lawmakers occurred during the aftermath of the Tax Reform Act of 1969. Responding to citizen dissatisfaction and to some of the obvious abuses of loopholes, Congress passed a comprehensive reform law that required all wealthy individuals to pay a minimum tax and excluded some low income groups from taxation. The law was complex and is not easily summarized, but it included these important features: (1)

corporate capital gains tax rate was raised from 25 percent to 30 percent; (2) excess bad debt write-offs for financial institutions were to be phased out (ending in 1988!); (3) multiple surtax exemptions were to be eliminated by 1975; (4) depletion allowance rates were reduced; (5) accelerated depreciation on equipment and buildings was reduced somewhat; (6) the 7 percent investment credit was eliminated; (7) the capital gains rate for individuals was raised to a maximum of 35 percent (previously the maximum rate was 25 percent); (8) the use of charity donations as a tax shelter were eliminated; and (9) a 50 percent maximum tax on individuals' *earnings* (wages, salary, commission) was instituted.

Although the Tax Reform Act has had some impact on tax expenditures, the changes have been minimal (see Table 10 for 1965 and 1972 rates on corporations, for example). The minimum tax provision forced a few millionaires, who had previously paid no tax, to pay a small tax—about 4 percent on incomes over $1 million and 3 percent on incomes over $200,000.[34] The 50 percent maximum tax on earned income was simply a subsidy for high paid executives, and contrary to expectations it did not stop them from investing in tax shelters (to reduce their tax even more). In addition to the marginal effectiveness of many provisions of the 1969 act, Congress enacted a law in 1971 that restored some of the tax benefits taken away in 1969. For example, depreciation deductions were increased and the investment credit of 7 percent was restored. And given more time, the wealthy will exert more pressure and reverse many of the provisions in the 1969 act and, perhaps, add some new loopholes.

Thus, because the wealthy—both individuals and corporations—possess disproportionate political power, they can over time expand loopholes and even reopen those closed by congressional zeal. After just two years, the 1971 act reversed several provisions of the 1969 act; and it can be expected that each successive skirmish in the never-ending war for wealth over the next years will expand other loopholes.

Delaying Tactics

Any good general knows that it is often wise to delay the battle and avoid an absolute resolution of conflict. Strategic retreats in the war for wealth are critical, for they give the wealthy time to overcome losses resulting from tax reform legislation. Probably most effective as delaying tactics are the phase-out clauses of many provisions designed to close tax loopholes. For example, the phase out of the excessive and accelerated bad debt write-off accorded financial institutions will not take full effect until 1988. By delaying the ultimate effect of a tax reform, the warriors of wealth beat a strategic retreat, but they have not lost the war. Instead, they have gained a considerable period of time in which to lobby against complete closure of the loopholes or to exert pressure for the opening of compensating loopholes.

Buying time is an important strategy in guerilla warfare. When out-maneuvered by public outrage or by congressional consciences, it is wise to retreat, delay, and regroup. And when the heat is off, the battle can be renewed.

THE CULTURE OF WEALTHFARE

In Chapter 7 we examine the commitment of Americans to Work and Welfare Ethics that place the poor, especially welfare recipients, in an extremely unfavorable light. These dual beliefs operate to create in the majority a perception that the poor and welfare recipients violate basic values of activism and achievement and are thus morally unworthy of anything but the most minimal welfare. The existence of these beliefs represents a diversion, for it keeps the majority focused on the activities and presumed welfare abuses of the poor who, after all, control only 5 percent of the total income and virtually none of the wealth. As such, the Work and Welfare Ethics are important elements of a culture of wealthfare, because they divert attention away from wealthfare payments.

Equally important to these diversionary beliefs, however, is a system of ideas that provides direct legitimation for wealthfare. Dominant values such as activism, progress, and materialism emphasize the appro-priateness of activities designed to expand material and capital wealth in American society. These values are made to seem the only desirable alternative by the value of morality, which makes other values absolutely right and proper. In the context of the political economy of wealthfare, activism, progress, and materialism have been translated into an evalua-tive belief that economic growth *should* continually occur, because only economic growth will enable individuals and society to progress and achieve ever-escalating levels of material well-being.

The belief that economic growth and expansion should occur is so well engrained into conventional political and economic wisdoms that few ever view this as anything other than fact. Wide acceptance of what can be termed the Growth Ethic has distorted perceptions about what actually exists and is possible in the economic and political worlds. These distortions are codified into two empirical beliefs that conveniently justify wealthfare and make it appear desirable, appropriate, and necessary. Through indirect subsidies of the economic marketplace and through tax expenditures, wealthfare receives wide support because of beliefs that (1) it is in the "national interest" and (2) it "trickles down" to all segments of the population.

National Interest

Government subsidy of the market could be visualized as violating the value of freedom from external governmental constraint. But this value is selectively invoked in American society. The welfare subsidy of the poor is considered to violate the Work Ethic and its underlying values. The subsidy of the affluent is defined as in the national interest.

Thus, *wealth*fare is typically justified as being needed to keep vital industries going, maintain employment for workers, reduce hardships of displaced employees, stimulate the economy, achieve national goals, or, almost unbelievably, maintain competition in key economic sectors.

Thus, wealthfare and welfare are viewed differently by most Americans. This indicates the differential application of dominant values and evaluative beliefs for different income groups. The selective application is possible because the public believes that welfare benefits *individuals* and so violates values such as "individualism" and "activism." In contrast, the public believes that subsidy to the affluent is to *organizations* and to *categories* of individuals (such as workers and investors), and so individuals in these subsidized organizations and categories avoid condemnation in terms of basic values. Further, the subsidy to the affluent provides work, whereas the subsidy to welfare recipients does not. This difference makes it possible to invoke the Work Ethic to mask any inconsistencies between the actual situation of the affluent and the dominant values of the society.

Humans are complex and creative symbolic creatures, and they are able to invoke values to condemn subsidy in one context, to applaud it in another. Belief in the national interest is one focal point around which this creative manipulation of values and beliefs occurs. The average citizen and worker is encouraged in this symbolic act by large corporations and unions that would lose a great deal if subsidies were exposed for what they are—wealthfare for the affluent. It is not surprising, then, that large corporations actively hail the national interest. For example, television commercials of large corporations on the government dole communicate the vital necessity of their enterprises. And Washington lobbyists of corporations and unions berate congressmen and the press about the hardships and economic problems that would inevitably ensue from any proposed cutback. Few lament similar cutbacks in welfare, because these are believed to be in the national interest.

Trickle Down

The trickle down belief provides further justification for subsidy of the organizations from which the affluent and wealthy derive their privilege. This belief is based on the assumption that measures to stimulate the economy will provide jobs for the poor, uneducated, nonunion workers. Subsidy is viewed as one way of realizing the equal opportunity implications of values such as activism, materialism, freedom, and individualism. Subsidy, after all, provides job opportunities to help people pull themselves up by their bootstraps and realize success through their individual efforts. Thus, the trickle down belief justifies subsidy to large corporations and unions under the illusion that such subsidy provides equal opportunity for the less affluent who, also by virtue of the subsidy, will now be given the opportunity to realize the imperatives of the Work · Ethic.

The national interest and trickle down beliefs do not correspond accurately to reality. It would be foolish to deny that subsidy of industry is not required, but the present *pattern* of subsidy is not necessarily in the national interest. Are all industries so vital? Cannot hardships on workers be mitigated in other ways? Is full employment in poorly managed and ecologically harmful organizations the best way to maintain full employment? Is stimulation of the economy more desirable than preventing rapid inflation?

Similarly, it would be a mistake to contend categorically that some benefits do not trickle down to the poor. But we question whether such benefits are proportional to need and whether the *pattern* of subsidy does not unnecessarily exacerbate inequality in America. How helpful is a job for an unskilled worker when the minimum wage is so low, when there is no assurance that the job will last, and when this worker is subjected to discrimination in the labor, commodities, and money markets of the economy?

Figure 1 The Culture and Structure of Wealthfare

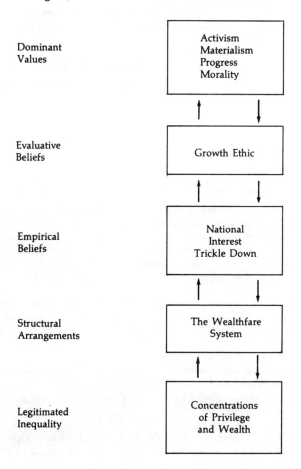

Dominant Values	Activism Materialism Progress Morality
Evaluative Beliefs	Growth Ethic
Empirical Beliefs	National Interest Trickle Down
Structural Arrangements	The Wealthfare System
Legitimated Inequality	Concentrations of Privilege and Wealth

In Figure 1, we summarize the relationships among the culture and structure of wealthfare. As the double arrows between values, evaluative beliefs, and empirical beliefs highlight, ideas form a cultural system that legitimates market subsidies and tax expenditures. Many of the ideas are kept alive and invoked as propaganda by the warriors for wealth. Most Americans accept them and thereby accept the wealthfare system. In turn, this wealthfare system perpetuates the privilege of the affluent and rich and in so doing maintains vast inequality in America.

NOTES

1. For a conservative estimate, see: Stanley S. Surrey, *Pathways to Tax Reform* (Cambridge, Mass.: Harvard University Press, 1973); for a more liberal estimate see: Philip M. Stern, *The Rape of the Taxpayer* (New York: Random House, 1972).

2. Roger A. Herriot and Herman P. Miller, "Changes in the Distribution of Taxes Among Income Groups, 1962–1968," (Mimeographed paper presented in August 1971 to American Statistical Association).

3. Actually, sales taxes can be deducted from federal income taxes, and in some states from state income taxes, and so the affluent pay a lower rate of sales tax, because their higher income brackets allows them to claim larger deductions and lower their tax brackets.

4. Surrey, *Pathways to Tax Reform*, pp. 92–93.

5. The exercise of stock options must eventually be paid when the stock is cashed in, but at a capital gains rate that, as we will see, represents a much lower tax rate.

6. As an example of how such a provision represents a wealthfare for the rich, the table below indicates which income groups owned most of the stock in the middle 1960s (things have not changed since then). These figures exclude corporate holdings:

Income Group	Percentage of Individually Held Corporate Stock
Top 1 percent	62
Top 5 percent	86
Top 20 percent	97
Middle 60 percent	3
Bottom 20 percent	Under 1

Source: Edward C. Budd, ed., *Inequality and Poverty* (New York: W. W. Norton, 1967), p. xxii.

7. Bonds also tend to be held by higher income individuals and large corporations. For example, Chase Manhattan and First National City Bank avoid $60 million per year in taxes with their bond holdings (See Stern, *Rape of the Taxpayer*, p. 65). Among individuals, the richest 7.6 percent of families derive 96 percent of tax benefits from bonds, the richest 1.2 percent derive 87 percent, and the richest 0.8 percent derive 76 percent of the tax benefits. (Stern, *Rape of the Taxpayer*, p. 64). Obviously, bond tax expenditures are wealthfare for the rich.

8. Formally, capital gains are defined as a deduction in the present tax structure. Previously they were defined as an exclusion. Some aspects of capital gains are still formally exclusions, as for example, when no capital gains are assessed on property transferred after death.

9. Surrey, *Pathways to Tax Reform*, p. 95.

10. At one time, this was considered as exclusion and in reality it still is; but the formal phrasing of current tax laws makes this exclusion a deduction.

11. See later section for a thorough discussion of the impact of capital gains tax rates—the biggest tax loophole of them all.

12. Surrey, *Pathways to Tax Reform*, p. 97.

13. The investment credit was introduced in 1962, suspended in 1966–1967. In 1969 it was finally withdrawn for good, but in 1971, it was reintroduced. In 1974, President

Ford proposed raising the investment credit to 10 percent, but the fate of this proposal has not been determined at this writing.

14. Stern, *Rape of the Taxpayer*, p. 96.

15. *Ibid.*, p. 95.

16. *Ibid.*, p. 94.

17. This analysis draws heavily on Stanley Surrey's more detailed analysis in *Pathways to Tax Reform*, pp. 60–81.

18. *Ibid.*, p. 61.

19. *Ibid.*, pp. 62–63.

20. This figure is a conservative guess, because it is impossible to collect data on these investments.

21. *Ibid.*, pp. 64–65.

22. *Ibid.*, p. 67.

23. *Ibid.*, p. 77.

24. Surrey, *Pathways to Tax Reform*, p. 77.

25. Some corporations avoid paying any taxes. In 1971, Alcoa Aluminum, Continental Oil, Gulf and Western, and McDonnell Douglas paid no taxes. In 1970, Bethlehem Steel, Consolidated Edison, National Steel, Republic Steel, and U.S. Steel paid no taxes. Other corporations pay very low rates. In 1971, for example, International Telephone and Telegraph (ITT) and Standard Oil of California paid virtually no taxes—5.0 percent and 1.6 percent respectively—on massive incomes. For additional data on the taxes of specific industries, see: Howard P. Tuckman, *The Economics of the Rich* (New York: Random House, 1973) and Stern, *Rape of the Taxpayer*.

26. Such inequality is maintained over generations because loopholes in the law allow the wealthy to pass much of their wealth on to their relatives. Space limitations have prevented us from examining these laws, but a careful examination of inheritance tax laws, estate tax codes, trust laws, and foundation regulations would reveal the legal loopholes used by the rich to keep their wealth over several generations. For a brief and highly readable source on these laws, see: Tuckman, *Economics of the Rich*, pp. 56–75.

27. *Ibid.*

28. Philip M. Stern, "How 381 Super-Rich Americans Managed Not to Pay a Cent in Taxes Last Year," *New York Times Magazine*, April 13, 1969.

29. Example taken from Surrey, *Pathways to Tax Reform*, p. 37.

30. *Ibid.*, p. 38–39.

31. This very proposal has passed the Senate several times, but fortunately was killed in conference committee with the House.

32. Tuckman, *Economics of the Rich*, pp. 72, 130, 138.

33. *Ibid.*, p. 130.

34. Tuckman, *Economics of the Rich*, p. 112; Stern, *Rape of the Taxpayer*, pp. 15–17.

7
THE WELFARE SYSTEM AND INEQUALITY

The term *welfare* is misleading, because it implies a system for assuring that people fare well in society. As the actual system for dealing with the poor has become institutionalized, it is not always clear that their well-being is promoted. As the counterpart to the *wealth*fare system, welfare in America often helps perpetuate poverty. The present system of welfare reflects the inability of the poor to exert sufficient power to redistribute income or to increase their relief. It also reveals the power of the affluent and rich to maintain a welfare system that simultaneously operates as wealthfare for the more privileged segments of the society. Welfare represents more than the expression of humanitarian values, although this expression should not be ignored. Welfare also represents the interests of the affluent and rich in an inexpensive labor pool. By inducing and forcing the poor to work in jobs for low wages and few fringe benefits, the wealthy can enjoy certain privileges at low cost. Welfare is much more than relief giving; it is also a governmental structure for intervention in the economic processes, especially those that bestow privilege on the affluent and wealthy.

THE HISTORICAL LEGACY OF WELFARE
For most of human history, poverty has been the fate of the masses. In contrast, poverty is the plight of only a minority in America, although this minority is large and totals perhaps as much as one-quarter of the population. Yet even with this dramatic change in the number of poor, the fundamental structure of the institutions established to deal with

the impoverished minority have not undergone basic changes. We will document specific shifts in the organizational structure of welfare in America. A longer view of welfare reveals remarkable continuity in the cultural premises and institutional arrangements of relief-giving in Anglo-American society.

Much of the current debate and controversy over welfare has occurred many times over during the last six hundred years. This long legacy of controversy over welfare and the current compromise solutions to these enduring controversies make the welfare system difficult to change. Institutional arrangements that emerged to accommodate the burgeoning capitalistic economic systems of western Europe during the fourteenth and fifteenth centuries have remained endemic to modern capitalistic economies. Many changes in the specific delivery system of relief have occurred as the nature of capitalism has changed, but a remarkable degree of continuity can also be observed. A brief portrayal of the historical legacy of welfare offers some clues to why the American system promotes inequality as much as it alleviates inequality.[1]

Relief-giving to the poor has always been a controversial subject. Fear of revolt, impulses of humanitarianism, the need for cheap labor, and rivalry between church and state have all influenced the profile of welfare over the past fifteen hundred years. The rivalry of church and state during the rise of capitalism in the fourteenth century marks a convenient beginning for a study of the historical antecedents to the Anglo-American system of welfare. It must be recognized, however, that most of the issues surrounding relief-giving during that period had been anticipated after the fall of the Roman Empire.

Prior to the emergence of extensive markets using money as the dominant medium of exchange, charity and relief-giving were primarily functions of the church, although local communities and private citizens often engaged in philanthropy. Then, as labor left the rural serfdoms of the crumbling feudal system, a *labor market* was created in the cities. Beggars had always been a problem and a subject of controversy, but this first urban proletariat in England and on the European continent posed a more severe problem of control. In an effort to restore control of labor to lords and to emerging capitalists, in 1349 Edward III issued an Ordinace of Laborers that outlawed the giving of relief by any citizen to able-bodied laborers. Shortly afterward, in 1351, Edward secured from Parliament a Statute of Laborers that set a maximum wage, required the unemployed to work for whoever demanded, restricted the travel of workers, and forbid charity to the able-bodied. In many ways, this statute explicitly set down what were to become basic features of modern welfare in America: residency requirements, support ceilings, and work requirements. Such laws enabled capitalists in need of cheap labor to have a ready supply, because able-bodied workers were forbidden to move and were forced to work for set wages. The severity of this system has been mitigated, but the basic profile of American welfare law is much the same as it was in England six hundred years ago.[2]

In the latter part of the fourteenth century and into the fifteenth, the rapid increase in British productivity, coupled with declines in the population from the Black Plague, created labor shortages. Peasant unrest and rebellions stemming from their eviction from agricultural lands resulted in further action by government to curb unrest and to keep a ready pool of inexpensive labor for capitalists. The statute of 1388 supplemented previous ordinances and statutes with two important features. (1) For the first time in secular law (the church had long made the distinction), the poor were distinguished in terms of their "impotence" and "able-bodiedness." (2) This distinction led to another—local communities were responsible for their "impotent poor." This requirement contained the legal origins of contemporary conceptions that local communities are responsible for the administration of welfare to "deserving poor." Not until 1495, when definitions of impotence were expanded to include some forms of vagrancy, and 1504, when those over sixty years of age were defined as impotent, did changes in these basic laws occur. The church still assumed much of the relief-giving burden, giving stability to the secular law and enabling the poor to avoid many of the restrictions of statutory law.

Subsequent changes in welfare policies were stimulated by activity on the European continent. In both Germany and Switzerland, changes —which were to be adopted by England many years later—were being made in the profile of relief-giving. By 1530, these changes included provisions that: (1) local citizens of "good standing" were "overseers" of poor relief; (2) these "overseers" had the power to "investigate" the homes and private lives of the poor; (3) the poor were educated, trained, and put to work whenever possible; (4) overseers censored the morality and life styles of the poor to make them repent their "evil" ways. In many ways, this system anticipated the modern American system of the 1950s and 1960s. Modern "eligibility workers" invaded homes of the poor to inspect their morals and local officials could force the poor to work and to secure job training.

During the later 1500s in England, many of these continental reforms were incorporated into English law. These changes culminated, in 1601, in the well-known Elizabethan Poor Laws, which were later supplemented by the 1662 Law of Settlement and Removal. These laws created a climate of relief-giving that has not changed appreciably to the present day and, equally important, they established some of the basic structural features of modern relief. Most notably, Elizabethan Poor Laws established that: (1) relief to the poor was to be based on need and moral evaluation; (2) relief was to be administered by local government; (3) the principal obligation for relief was to fall on relatives; (4) the recipient of relief was to have well-established residency in the community giving the relief.

These provisions, coupled with previous laws that distinguished categories of poor—the able-bodied and the impotent—and that forced the poor
to work when employment was offered, anticipated contemporary American attitudes toward welfare as well as some of the concrete structural
arrangements of the American welfare establishment.

This British system of relief met many of the economic requirements
of early capitalism in seventeenth century England. Relief laws kept the
poor in the labor market by prohibiting migration and forcing the able-
bodied to work for fixed wages. In this way capitalists, whose profits
depended on a pool of cheap labor, were able to generate high profits
and the capital that led to further expansion of the economy. The extent
to which this welfare system was established to meet the economic
requirements of capitalism can be seen by examining the resistance of
the economic elite to an alternative initiated in the district of Speenhamland and generally adopted by Parliament in 1795.

Basically, the Speenhamland proposal was for a minimum cost-of-
living wage that was tied to a "bread scale" or cost of living index. Wages
were to be subsidized by local governments to keep them abreast of
the actual costs of living. The Speenhamland plan, adopted by Parliament
in 1795, was the first national program of what are now termed guaranteed annual income policies. Unfortunately, this plan was never effectively implemented because of the intense resistance of the economic
elite. The program was considered disruptive of the natural laws of supply
and demand in the labor and commodities market, and it was intensely
criticized by the ideological spokesmen of laissez-faire capitalism. Adam
Smith argued—as have the critics of contemporary income guarantees—that the system would bring higher taxes, higher prices, lower
private wages, sloth, idleness, and continued poverty. By the 1830s, the
income allowance program was formally abandoned, although in fact
it had hardly ever been used. And in its place came the Poor Law
Amendment Act of 1834. That law established a national policy of welfare
for the impotent and tossed the able-bodied into the workhouse where
conditions were so bad that most preferred to seek work for low wages
in the private job market. Further, although national policy guided the
giving of relief, it was administered at the local community level.

By the middle of the nineteenth century, the English system of relief
kept the poor from starving while forcing the "able poor" onto the job
market. As such, the system did indeed give relief, but it did not enable
the poor to fare well in the commodities or labor markets. In fact, the
workhouse test represented *wealth*fare for the capitalists, because it
forced many of the poor to work for low wages to avoid the workhouses.
By paying low wages, the owners of production were able to increase
their profits, but equally important, prices on many goods and services
were kept lower than they would have been otherwise. Government
interference in the labor market—despite the denials of classical economists—thus subsidized the rich owners and the more affluent buyers

of goods and services. It is in this sense, then, that welfare became a form of wealthfare in Anglo-American societies. And these features of the British system were to be incorporated into American welfare programs.

THE EMERGENCE OF WELFARE IN AMERICA
The Early System of Relief

Many of the traditions of relief-giving to the poor in America were originally imported from England.[3] Only the most destitute—the orphaned and the handicapped—were to receive charity from the philanthropy of *private* individuals and organizations in *local* communities. The workhouse, with its severe and harsh work requirements and subsistence levels of food, shelter, and clothing, became the principal means for inducing or forcing the able-bodied "indolent" to contrive ways to support themselves.

These traditions were well entrenched in the structure of communities in early colonial America: (1) relief was a local community matter; (2) relief was only for the most deserving, and even then it was defined as charity; (3) relief for those able to work was given under such unpleasant conditions that any alternative to welfare was defined as desirable. Such a situation was easily legitimated by dominant values. The values of activism, achievement, materialism, and progress and the prevailing morality, fostered the belief that everyone must actively pursue material sustenance if individual betterment and societal progress were to ensue. Further, the values of freedom and individualism stressed that individuals were to be free from constraint in pursuing success in the land of opportunity. During this early colonial period a Work Ethic became codified and began to shape people's perceptions and actions toward those who did not derive their income from work activities. This ethic relegated to the purgatory of the workhouse or the patronage of charity those who would not, or could not, work for a living.

The relationship between the states and the federal governments was also important in creating the structure and culture of relief-giving in early America. Buttressed and legitimated by the values of freedom as codified in "states rights" evaluative beliefs, the federal government remained uninvolved in the internal affairs of the states. The federal government was eventually to become involved in many internal state functions, including relief-giving. But this involvement was kept as indirect as was possible, because of the influence of states rights beliefs as translated into a federalist system of national government. Indeed, charity and relief were to remain functions of the states and local communities, as was reaffirmed by President Pierce in 1854:[4]

[If Congress should] make provision for such objects, the fountains of charity will be dried up at home, and the several states, instead of bestowing their own means on the social wants of their own people, may themselves, through the strong

temptation, which appeals to states as individuals, become humble supplicants for the bounty of the Federal Government, reversing their true relation to this union.

Up to the 1930s, this pattern of federal uninvolvement in relief and its consequent relegation to states and local communities was to prevail. This early system, legitimated by dominant values and prevalent evaluative beliefs, was to constrain subsequent development of the welfare establishment. Although the federal government was to assume some of the financial burden of welfare, and for brief periods much of the administrative load, the pattern of relief-giving had already been established by the 1930s. As in early relief-giving in England, this pattern served the economic interests of organizations and individuals who desired inexpensive labor. At the same time, it assured that no effective national system of income redistribution could be established.

The Great Depression and Welfare[5]
From 1929 to 1932, the United States sank rapidly into a deep economic depression, and millions of people could not find work. Yet, even in the face of widespread unemployment and poverty, groups with an economic interest in a cheap labor pool and low taxes effectively stalled federal intervention into the relief-giving activities of local communities. As late as 1931, President Hoover proclaimed, "I am opposed to any direct or indirect government dole—our people are providing against distress from unemployment in true American fashion."[6]

Despite Hoover's convictions and the optimistic proclamations of local officials and community organizations such as Community Chest, municipal governments and private agencies were overburdened by rapidly escalating relief requirements. Citizens were frustrated by the inability of government to respond, and civil disorder in the streets of major urban areas escalated as the unemployed began to aggressively demand some financial relief. Thus, by 1932, a severe financial and political crisis faced leaders of local communities as the cities went bankrupt and their residents became increasingly disaffected and restive.

Out of this economic and political climate, Franklin D. Roosevelt fashioned the new Democratic coalition that was to shape federal policies for the next fifteen years. As soon as he took office in March of 1933, Roosevelt moved quickly to intervene directly in the economic affairs of regions, states, and local communities—federal regulation unprecedented in American history. Although the Civilian Conservation Corps and the Works Progress Administration achieved high visibility as relief measures, the most effective and enduring measure was the Federal Emergency Relief Administration, which dramatically changed the nature of relief-giving in the United States. The provisions of this act, and the administrative structure it established, allowed the federal government to provide grants to the states and communities for their use in relief activities. Thus, for the first time, the federal government intervened directly in the welfare activities of the states and local communities. By 1935, however, pressure to restore the previous relief system was evident. Even Roosevelt maintained that "the Federal Government must and shall quit this business of relief."[7] Shortly thereafter, in 1935, the one and a half million aged, disabled, and orphaned who were receiving federal relief were turned back to the states and communities. Further measures in 1935 put others back to work at a "security wage" that was higher than relief payments but lower than prevailing wages—a strong affirmation of dominant values and, coincidentally, of the need of the economic elite for an inexpensive labor pool. At the same time, the Social Security Act of 1935, which provided old age pensions and unemployment insurance (to be effective in 1942), established the basic structure of the federal government's future intervention in welfare. This act, which was similar to its predecessors in England, allowed the federal government to provide "grants and aids" to states for certain "categories" of "impotent" poor, such as the aged, blind, orphaned, and dependent children (with one parent). However, for the able-bodied poor who were not able to find employment in the years preceding World War II and who could not secure local relief, the federal government made no provision[8]—thus assuring economic interests of a large pool of desperately needy labor.

Between 1935 and 1939, most states took advantage of the categorical grants and aids provided by the Social Security Act. During this period the basic structure of the contemporary welfare establishment was erected. (1) The states were allowed to set their own grant levels—thereby assuring the large disparities in assistance that persist to the present day. (2) Because the federal government made no provisions for able-bodied individuals who could not find work, the states similarly failed to provide relief assistance. (Only when the Social Security Act was amended in 1961 were families with an unemployed father eligible for federal aid.) (3) Few dependent children initially got aid, because states were slow to set programs into motion; but when Aid to Families with Dependent Children (AFDC) was established, the "no man in the house rule" (a rule only recently changed) was strictly enforced. (4) All the states set up "work requirements" for mothers in AFDC programs—thereby assuring another pool of low-wage industrial and domestic labor. In this way, states and communities regained control of their welfare programs, with the financial backing of the federal government. When the present system is compared to early relief systems in England, the parallels are clear.

The Abusive Years, 1940–1960
The structure of relief-giving changed little between 1940 and 1960. Millions of people in dire need of assistance were denied aid by the restrictive administrative policies of state and local welfare bureaucracies. For example, the able-bodied male unemployed, even when the head

of a family, were kept off the welfare rolls. Although the 1961 Social Security Act allowed federal grants and aids to states for male heads of families, less than thirty states had taken advantage of that money by the end of the 1960s. The restrictions for welfare varied from state to state, and so did the amounts for various categories of recipients. For example, southern states had consistently lower payments to fewer categories of needy than western, northeastern, or north central states. This situation has not changed even today. Welfare payments from state to state, and in some instances, from county to county within a state, still vary enormously. One apparent reason for this variability is the desire of state and county officials to keep payments below the lowest prevailing wage in a region—thereby forcing or inducing people to work in order to survive. A 1969 study reports that the state-by-state rank order correlation coefficient between agricultural wages (typically the lowest in any region) and relief payments was .75 in 1951 and .84 in 1960.[9] These data indicate that the needs of economic interests probably dictate welfare policies as much as the needs of the impoverished—a situation that has changed little since the early days of capitalism in England. By tying welfare payments to the interests of economic elites, welfare policies have effectively prevented income redistribution in America.

As tragic as the variability and sparsity of welfare payments were (and are today), perhaps more abusive were the practices of welfare bureaucracies designed to keep people off welfare. Variations in welfare policies make it difficult to generalize, but some abusive practices are so widespread that we emphasize them:

(1) In contrast to Social Security and the Veterans' Administration, welfare bureaucracies have never advertised their benefits to the public. Such public information campaigns are assumed to violate a Work Ethic by encouraging people to withdraw from the labor pool and live on the government dole. Almost one-half of those eligible for welfare never apply—and ignorance of the benefits is at least one of the causes for this statistic.[10] This has been compounded by the unnecessarily complicated and voluminous rules and regulations which, it is said, only trained welfare workers can interpret and understand—a myth that has kept welfare policies shrouded in mystery.

(2) When the impoverished do apply for welfare, they are often deliberately subjected to intimidation and abuse by local officials trying to discourage applications. Eligibility workers ask hostile questions, clerks and officials are aggressive, applicants suffer long waits in crowded rooms, and armed guards are often posted at entrances. When faced with these abuses, the poor, who are already ill at ease in the welfare bureaucracy because of their own commitment to dominant values and the Work Ethic, have been discouraged from coming back and subjecting themselves to further assaults on their self-esteem and dignity.[11]

(3) Because county governments are left to administer their own pro-grams without fear of reprisals by the federal government, applicants are often treated arbitrarily. The most common practice is to turn down an applicant, even though the applicant meets eligibility requirements. Between 1940 and 1960 there were no formal appeals channels. Welfare applicants, who are kept in the dark about the rules, have had little choice but to accept their fate. Another arbitrary practice has been to cut off benefits without warning or explanation. A national study con-ducted in 1961 revealed that 34 percent of closed cases were still eligible for welfare and that 12 percent of all cases—8 percent white and 21 percent black—had been closed for "other reasons." Careful examination revealed that in nearly one-half of the cases the other reason was an "unsuitable home" (a vague administrative license that allows eligibility workers to arbitrarily cut off benefits).[12]

(4) Welfare bureaucracies often under-budget relief payments. The result is that recipients often receive less money than they are entitled to under existing administrative regulations. Because recipients are not allowed access to the rules, it has been difficult for them to know if they are being cheated. Under-budgeting makes living on welfare so difficult that many recipients seek work, even at a below-subsistence wage. This procedure, intentionally or otherwise, reduces the welfare rolls.

(5) Finally, between 1940 and 1960 welfare recipients had to endure invasions of their privacy. AFDC mothers were asked questions about their morals and sex lives; midnight raids were made without warrants on the homes of AFDC mothers homes to check on whether there was a "man in the house"; and welfare investigators have been allowed to keep track of the daily routines of recipients. Such abuses went unresisted because welfare administrators had the power to threaten termination of benefits. Thus, recipients were coerced into being accomplices to violations of their civil rights.

Abusive practices such as these became typical in welfare bureaucracies between 1940 and 1960. All of these practices were designed for a simple purpose: to keep people off of welfare and in the job market. In some cases, welfare administrators were simply responding to political and economic pressure for an inexpensive and seasonal labor supply; in other cases, administrators were reacting to public pressure to enforce the Work Ethic for "people's own good"; and in still other instances, welfare workers were simply imposing their own versions of morality on their clients. It would be incorrect, of course, to assume that welfare adminis-trators and workers were not concerned about their needy clients; many undoubtedly were concerned and conscientiously sought to meet the needs of the poor within the guidelines of federal and state laws. Yet abuse was widespread and deterred at least one-half of those who were eligible from seeking assistance. Undoubtedly there are some among the poor whose beliefs in a Work Ethic kept them from applying for welfare. But all too frequently it was the practices of the welfare bureaucracy that kept the relief rolls down and an inexpensive supply of labor available. The poor were kept poor, whether on sparse relief payments or in low paying jobs, and the system of inequality in America was maintained.

The Welfare Explosion, 1960–1975

Since the middle 1960s, the number of poor on welfare has grown dramatically. Political pressures from a hostile urban population, which had been partially mobilized by the War on Poverty programs of the Great Society, have resulted in court challenges of many of the restrictive and abusive policies of the welfare establishment. In response to a suit initiated by Office of Economic Opportunity attorneys in 1968, a three-judge federal panel in Atlanta struck down laws that required AFDC mothers to be willing and ready to work. In 1968 the "man in the house" rule for welfare mothers was declared unconstitutional by the Supreme Court. In 1970 the Supreme Court ruled that welfare recipients have a constitutional right to an appeals hearing before welfare officials if the recipient's benefits are terminated. Midnight raids by welfare officials were also declared unconstitutional. And in 1969 even daytime visits were declared unconstitutional by a panel of federal judges in New York, although the Supreme Court subsequently overturned this ruling.

At the same time that OEO was successfully working toward elimination of some welfare abuses through the courts, welfare rights activist groups were springing up all over the country, and a national parent organization—the National Welfare Rights Organization—was formed. The NWRO collects dues and has used these financial resources to collect and disseminate information to recipients about their welfare rights. It has also financed suits against states and communities that abuse the rights of welfare recipients.

Again, as in England in the fourteenth century, the relaxation in welfare restrictions was largely a means for "cooling out" restive urban masses without making major structural changes in patterns of urban government, school segregation, union exclusion, and housing discrimination. The expanding welfare rolls posed a threat to economic interests in need of cheap labor and violated the public's commitment to a Work Ethic, but they were less threatening to most Americans than major changes in housing policies, schools, patronage systems in government, and discriminatory practices in the economy. Reorienting the welfare establishment proved to be the least costly way of dealing with a large and concentrated population that was no longer willing to suffer poverty in a society of abundance.

It is difficult to be sure that a direct causal relation exists, but the rise in the number of welfare recipients corresponds to a slight increase in the bottom income fifth's share of the total income. This share rose from 4.9 percent of the total in 1960 to 5.7 percent in 1968, then dropped to 5.4 percent in 1973 (see Chapter 3). This modest increase may indicate that the increase in Welfare transfer payments created some income redistribution. But the increase is not large enough to be considered a change in basic patterns of inequality (and it might simply be a statistical artifact). A considerable amount of suffering may have been reduced by reorientation of welfare bureaucracies, but patterns of inequality have not been significantly altered. Relief payments are still very low, often forcing or inducing people to work for low wages in ungratifying jobs with few fringe benefits; there are still enormous variation in payments; and recipients are still subjected to extensive monitoring.

The beneficial changes in the welfare system should not be underemphasized, but the present structure still seems to reflect the economic needs of the affluent and rich as much as the needs of the poor. It is in this sense that welfare policies operate as wealthfare for the affluent and the rich and expose the poor to the vicissitudes of the present economic system in America. Some critics have charged that this situation represents "free enterprise for the poor, socialism for the rich." Although this may be an overstatement, it does emphasize that wealthfare often *protects* the affluent and rich from economic hardship, whereas welfare sometimes exposes the poor to the most damaging features of capitalistic markets. This relationship between patterns of economic organization and welfare policies is centuries old, and its consequences for American society require some elaboration.

WELFARE, ECONOMIC ORGANIZATION, AND INEQUALITY
Welfare exposes the poor to the maladies of capitalist forms of economic organization in two ways: (1) it forces or induces them to compete for low-paying jobs in a cyclical labor market; and (2) it keeps relief benefits and wages low, with the result that the poor are at a disadvantage in the goods and service markets of the economy. Probably the best way to visualize these two processes is to review the plight of the poor in the basic markets of the American economy.

Economic Cycles and the Labor Market
The operation of a complex economy, such as we have in the United States, is highly unpredictable. Capitalist economies are subject to cycles of high production and employment, followed by decreased production and employment which, after a period of market readjustments and corrective actions by government, lead to increased production and employment. Capitalistic economies are thus subject to boom and bust cycles that result in periodic economic recessions and, as has happened on several occasions in American history, deep economic depressions.[13]

During these periodic recessions, the inequality generated by the current structuring of the labor market becomes dramatically evident. Although it is easy to find exceptions to blanket generalizations, it is not completely unreasonable to assert that those who are fired first during recessions are those who can least afford to be out of work. Although white-collar workers and unionized blue-collar workers also feel the bite of economic recessions, they have been, especially over the past few years, better prepared financially to cope with them. The unskilled and poorly paid workers, who have no unions, are hit hard by recessions, and they are forced to suffer the degradation that Americans impose on those who seek welfare. At any given time in America, one-fifth of all welfare recipients are heads of families who have been laid off because of economic cutbacks. The figure tends to rise during periods of recession even though many of the poor steadfastly refuse to go on welfare, preferring instead to exhaust limited savings and to incur extensive debts at high rates of interest.

Thus, the bottom income groups are the first to suffer from inevitable economic cycles; and it is they who, because of debts incurred during their unemployment, continue to suffer even after they resume work. The more affluent worker, protected by savings or the benefits provided by unions, is able to avoid extensive debt and experiences faster financial recovery when unemployment ends. It is the poor, then, who are most likely to suffer in the labor market of a free-enterprise economic system; the affluent and wealthy have more ways of avoiding and forestalling these traumas.

Competition in the Labor Market

It has often been noted that the American economy is entering a stage of *postindustrialization.* This term indicates that the labor force in American society is being used less for production of goods and more for the provision of services. Service occupations have two features that distinguish them from other jobs: (1) they are defined as requiring more education; and (2) they are white-collar—the work is more mental than manual. Education in mental skills is becoming the equivalent of the blue-collar worker's union card. Such education increases access to well-paying jobs, enhances chances of reasonably steady employment, and diminishes competition for jobs.

Poorly educated and relatively unskilled workers are disadvantaged in an economy that is highly unionized in its productive sector and professionalized in its service sphere. As the extractive and productive sectors increasingly automate their operations, the unskilled worker finds it increasingly difficult to get a job, because the number of steady menial jobs continues to decrease. The labor force has been increasing at an annual rate of one and a half million. The worker who is not protected by education or union membership faces severe competition for the remaining jobs. This high demand for unskilled jobs keeps wages low and forces the unskilled worker to compete with peers for jobs that offer low pay and—because of the effect of inevitable economic cycles— little security.

The government has let this situation persist, preferring to maintain the free enterprise mechanism in the unskilled labor market. Union workers and white-collar professionals are likely to enjoy the benefits of government support of their industries through government purchases or cash subsidies that increase the probability of reasonably steady employment even during recessions. These industries receive another subsidy from the federal government's hands-off policy for the unskilled. Because the market mechanism operates in this sector of the labor market, inexpensive labor is available to industry. A further subsidy is provided for the affluent and industry by welfare policies that barely keep the poor alive when they are not needed but force them to work for low wages when they are needed. The regulation and subsidy of the unskilled labor market is for the benefit of the affluent, who prefer inexpensive maids and gardeners, and for big industry, which periodically needs inexpensive labor. Welfare policies and the reluctance of the government to create jobs force the poor onto the job market, where they must compete with each other and thereby lower wages.

Wages in the Labor Market
The relatively high demand for the skilled services of white-collar workers, plus selective pump-priming of corporations with defense and civilian contracts, have kept the wages of white-collar workers comparatively high. Similar pump-priming and other forms of subsidy by the federal government of blue-collar industries, coupled with the collective bargaining power of unions, have kept wages of most unionized workers relatively high. In contrast to these groups of workers are the hundreds of thousands of unskilled whose only protection is the federal minimum wage. The current minimum wage of two dollars per hour cannot provide even a subsistence level of living for the head of a family who works forty hours a week for the entire year. The plight of these workers is dramatically underscored by the fact that, of the over eight million families who received welfare in 1974, about one-quarter were headed by persons who worked full time but whose wages could not support their families.[14]

One solution to this situation is to raise the minimum wages to a level allowing an above subsistence living standard. However, just getting the wage to $2 per hour has been difficult. When the $2 rate was first proposed in 1971, the Nixon administration declared the plan inflationary and opted for a gradual escalation of the wage to this level in 1974. Whether the justification for keeping wages low is inflation or some other rationalization, the federal government has always been reluctant to adjust the minimum wage to keep pace with the cost of living. At the same time, however, the federal government has encouraged collective bargaining by unions to raise wages. Even in 1971, when the Nixon administration decried as inflationary union demands for wage increases in several key industries, the government allowed settlements that dramatically increased the wages and fringe benefits of union workers. Tragically, nonunion and unskilled workers lack the political clout to pressure the federal government into assuring them the same wage benefits as those enjoyed by the better organized union workers. And so nonunions and unskilled workers are left to compete in a labor market decreasingly in need of the unskilled and uneducated.

The Money Market and Inequality

The money market in a modern society is complex and defies easy analysis. However, by focusing on how this market contributes to the patterns of inequality described in Chapters 2 and 3, we can simplify our analytical task. We can derive a fairly accurate picture of the inequalities built into the structure of this market by focusing on two basic processes. (1) What options are available to various income groups to make more money with their money? (2) What options for borrowing money are available to various income groups seeking credit?

In a classic free-enterprise system, the interest rates for money are set in the marketplace in accordance with the laws of supply and demand. However, the government—in an effort to create stability in the money market—enacted what is now known as Federal Reserve Regulation Q. This regulation limits the amounts of interest that commercial banks, savings and loan associations, and mutual savings banks can pay their depositors. Particularly important are the limitations on commercial banks, because close to one third of all savings deposits in these banks are held by individuals with incomes of less than $5,000. Equally significant, a clear majority of this one third of depositors hold no other financial assets and thus have no other way to make money with their savings.[15]

For example, the interest rate on savings in banks hovers at around 5 percent; for small depositors in savings and loans, it is 5.5 to 6 percent. For larger depositors in savings and loans as well as other savings institutions, considerably higher interest rates are available. But more significant, the wealthy have alternative investment opportunities not available to small investors. For example, the wealthy can invest in tax free municipal bonds. The income from these, coupled with the tax exemption these bonds allow, yields high rates of return for high income purchasers. Or, the wealthy can invest in somewhat more risky ventures, such as oil exploration (the risks are greatly diminished by government subsidies), real estate trusts, and housing syndicates.[16] The favorable tax deductions, depreciations, and exemptions associated with investments in these areas enable the rich to derive a high return on these investments.

The poor cannot earn money with their money, for several reasons: (1) they are unaware of the opportunities; (2) they cannot afford to hire consultants and accountants who can advise them of opportunities; (3) they do not have sufficient savings to qualify for a share in these profitable investments; and (4) their incomes and tax brackets are too low to qualify for tax deductions allowed by investments in these enterprises.

The more affluent exert pressure for enactment of laws that would permit high brokerage fees on small investments and would limit small denomination bonds.[17] In contrast, the government appeals to the patriotism of wage earners to encourage them to buy low yield savings bonds. Clearly there is discrimination against the small investor. It is curious that federal regulations and policies curtail open competition in the one market where the less affluent could benefit from free enterprise. It can be reasonably argued that the less affluent in America experience the ravages of free enterprise in the labor market but are excluded from some of its potential benefits in the money market.

When the less affluent seek to borrow money they again face discrimination. Lending money is big business in the United States. Outstanding credit to the public in a given year totals about one hundred forty billion dollars.[18] About one-half of all families in America have outstanding installment debts and these debts are as frequent among the rich as among the poor.[19] As our earlier analysis of the tax system would indicate, however, this should not be surprising. It costs money to borrow money. The interest rates paid by different income groups and the ways that interest can be used to reduce taxes for various income groups are examples of the inequality built into the structure of the credit market. When the poor borrow on the credit market, they usually lose money; when the rich borrow, they usually save money.

When seeking credit, a consumer is confronted by a range of lenders in the market place: (1) the commercial loan section of a bank; (2) the installment loan department of this bank; (3) credit unions; (4) credit card companies; (5) finance companies; (6) the dealer selling a good or commodity; and (7) loan sharks. The simple interest rates charged by these various lenders in 1974 ranged from 10 percent or 11 percent to 300 to 400 percent. It is especially important, in analyzing inequities built into the credit market, to be aware that the affluent borrower can sometimes get a loan from the commercial loan department of a bank at the prime (lowest current) interest rate—about 10 to 12 percent in 1974. Failing this, an affluent borrower can get credit in the installment loan department, at interest averaging about 18 percent in 1974. Consumers attached to large organizations or affiliated with unions can usually borrow money at 12 percent from their credit unions. Borrowers with good credit ratings are usually charged 18 percent by credit card companies, loan companies, and dealers selling goods and commodities (the latter simply sell their contracts to loan companies and banks). But those whose incomes are insufficient to command good credit ratings find that credit cards are less available, and they are charged 40 percent by loan companies. Retail stores raise their rates dramatically or do not lend at all to these customers. Too often, the poor must turn to the loan sharks, whose rates vary from 100 percent to 400 percent and whose tactics of solicitation and collection are rarely legal.

In the credit market, a borrower's credit rating is critical in securing loans at low interest rates. There are several thousand local credit bureaus in America, and they provide lenders with the ratings of potential borrowers. These credit bureaus assign points for various characteristics. For example, professional occupations are worth extra points, occupations that provide tenure and pay well are worth additional points, lengthy residence in an area is worth some more points, being married adds still more, having bank accounts helps some more, and maintaining a stock of credit cards helps provide additional points. A borrower loses points if outstanding loans to finance companies or jewelry stores exist. A credit rating is determined by adding up an individual's total points (less any minuses). Various lenders have their own systems of charging interest rates that correspond to different point totals, but in general, the more points, the lower the interest to be charged.

There is an obvious logic to this procedure: those who have a high capacity to repay are able to borrow at low interest rates. The poor are thus left to a market mechanism that brands them as poor risks—a safe assumption in light of their situation in the free enterprise labor market—and thus forces them to pay more for money. Perhaps this procedure seems fair, until we recall the federal government subsidies of low interest loan guarantees to many large corporations in both industry and agriculture—the recent Lockheed loan guarantee of $250 million is unusual only for its size. Further, through the Federal Reserve mechanism, the federal government regulates the prime interest rate for affluent borrowers. That regulation has little impact on the 40 percent interest charged by loan companies and the 100 percent to 400 percent charged by loan sharks. The poor are left to fend for themselves in the credit market, while the federal government keeps a watchful eye on the interest charged the more affluent and rich segments of the society.

A further subsidy for the wealthy, and to some extent for the middle-income borrower, comes from the income tax laws—interest paid on loans in a given year can be deducted from income tax for that year. This provision favors the affluent who can save money by borrowing large sums, deducting the interest from their taxes, and lowering their total tax bill. This option is of little help to the poor, for several reasons: (1) they are not in sufficiently high income brackets for interest deductions to make much difference; (2) they cannot afford tax consultants who can advise them of the maximum utility to be gained by a given interest deduction; (3) the government provides them with the simplified standard deduction, which simplifies tax preparation but blinds them to many legitimate deductions; and (4) the poor have little knowledge about what they can deduct, and they are dealing with a tax system that is unnecessarily complex.

The Commodities and Goods Market

It has been estimated that the poor buy around $30 billion worth of goods—food, housing, clothing, and other commodities—in a given year. However, the poor are not always able to get full value for their purchases. This situation is inequitable, especially because those who have little money are the ones who need to get the most for their money. Because the poor must inevitably pay out most if not all of their incomes for housing, food, and clothing, failure to get their money's worth in these commodities has far greater impact than failure of the affluent to get the best bargain in new cars or jet flights.

One reason the poor pay more is that they do not have the mobility or flexibility enjoyed by the affluent in the marketplace. The poor, trapped in inner-city slums or rural hamlets, cannot shop around for housing, clothing, and food. Even when various options are available, the poor have less opportunity to compare prices in stores at different locations. Transportation for comparison shopping is costly and time consuming. And many justifiably fear they would face discrimination if they were to venture out of their neighborhoods. In contrast, middle-class and rich buyers have cars and ample money for gasoline and can shop and compare in a relatively competitive market. The immobility of the poor makes them subject to the monopolistic practices of local merchants, and so the poor must pay more money, item for item, for food, housing, and clothing.[20] One study documented that the rents paid by the poor, particularly in racial and ethnic ghettos, tend to be about 8 percent greater than rents paid by whites outside of ghettos.[21] Another study revealed that in the early 1960s black residents paid, on the average, $15 a month more than whites for equivalent housing—a considerable amount of money for the times, especially on a limited budget. These studies demonstrate the extent to which the poor must endure the disadvantages of a free enterprise system, while the affluent are able to experience some of its benefits.

This situation is compounded by still another inequity. Because the poor have little surplus, they cannot stock up on goods during sales. Their incomes come in small quantities, such as weekly paychecks, and there is little left for savings. And so the poor must live from hand to mouth, shopping frequently and unable to take advantage of sales.

And finally, the poor must pay large sales taxes on their purchases in most states. Sales taxes are highly regressive because all income groups pay at the same rate. A 5 percent sales tax is a significant bite into a small income but merely an inconvenience for someone in a high income bracket. Furthermore, the affluent can avoid the full impact of the sales tax because they are in income brackets that allow them to deduct sales taxes from their federal income taxes. The poor must pay the full 5 percent, because their incomes are not sufficiently high to make sales tax deductions meaningful. Thus, not only do the poor pay more sales tax, item for item, than the affluent, but the sales tax represents a greater proportion of their limited incomes.

In sum, the welfare system perpetuates poverty by keeping direct relief payments at or below subsistence and by inducing or forcing the poor to seek the only slightly higher levels of income in a highly competitive and unstable job market. And, low wages and relief benefits place the poor at a disadvantage in the money and commodities markets. Welfare policies can only be understood in relation to their consequences for economic processes. The more affluent and rich receive wealthfare from the low wages paid the poor, while the poor are kept dependent on a welfare system that exposes them to the unpleasant side of capitalism.

There has been growing recognition that something is wrong with the current welfare system, which costs billions, does not eliminate poverty, and alienates the poor. This dissatisfaction has yet to be translated into concrete changes in the basic structure of the welfare system, but it has stimulated a search for alternatives. Those suggested so far unfortunately resemble practices in the district of Speenhamland during the eighteenth century in England.

NEW ALTERNATIVES TO WELFARE: THE GUARANTEED ANNUAL INCOME

The most likely alternative to the present welfare system is the guaranteed income, or negative income tax, which would set an income floor for all families and individuals. The federal government would subsidize the difference between a hypothetical income floor and actual income, thereby assuring people of enough to live on. The advantages of such a program are many. (1) Much of the current state and county welfare bureaucracy would be eliminated, and the workers in these bureaucracies would begin performing community services instead of surveillance. (2) Many of the abuses of the rights and dignity of the poor would be eliminated by use of a spot checking or auditing system, such as the IRS uses for *wealth*fare recipients. (3) If the income floor were set at an adequate level and then constantly adjusted upward to take account of inflation, abject poverty would be eliminated and some modest degree of income redistribution would occur.

The program also has disadvantages. (1) The costs would be high, at least $30 billion per year in 1975 dollars. These costs could be financed by eliminating tax expenditures and lowering wealthfare payments to the affluent—a feat which would make for a more equitable distribution of income without cutting into existing federal expenditures, but which would be resisted by the affluent majority. (2) The program could be inflationary, because it would increase direct federal expenditures. This problem could be overcome by reducing tax expenditures, which, despite their indirect nature, are as inflationary as direct expenditures. (3) If the guaranteed income were constructed through tax laws and agencies, then all of the problems associated with tax expenditures would apply to the guaranteed income. The public might find an income guarantee more acceptable if it were presented as a negative tax—after all, they are used to getting their subsidies through the tax system. But it would be preferable to make income guarantees direct expenditures, lest the negative tax to the poor be used as a justification and lever for giving new benefits to the affluent. If all tax expenditures were converted to direct expenditure items, then the costs of income guarantees might not seem so high, especially if state sales and income taxes, as well as local property taxes, were no longer used to finance welfare.

But probably the greatest disadvantage of the guaranteed annual income cannot be easily overcome, because it is built into the cultural, political, and economic realities of American society. It is likely that Congress, in an effort to maintain a pool of low-wage labor, would make the guaranteed annual income so low that it would not provide an adequate standard of living for the poor. It is also likely that Congress would legislate work requirements for some categories of recipients, to keep them from violating the Work Ethic. And finally, a guaranteed annual income—even one set too low—could be heralded as a major welfare reform and used to avoid equitable redistribution of the income, while simultaneously perpetuating rather than eradicating poverty.

Probably the best way to appreciate these structural realities is to examine the now abandoned but once trumpeted welfare reform, or Family Assistance Plan, of the Nixon administration. For a family of four (note that no provision was made for single individuals) a minimum income of $1600 was to have been guaranteed, with $899 more in the form of food stamps also guaranteed. When this program was originally proposed in 1971, the bare subsistence living costs for an urban family of four were around $5,500 to $6,500 according to Labor Department statistics (a somewhat higher figure was established by NWRO). Thus, the total guaranteed income of the Nixon Family Assistance Plan—$2,494—was at least $3,000 short of what was necessary for subsistence in 1971. Furthermore, work and job training requirements were mandatory for those receiving income guarantees—and so a continued supply of inexpensive labor was assured.

In 1974, President Ford circulated a draft of a guaranteed income plan. This plan would completely eliminate traditional welfare—aid to dependent children, food stamps, supplemental security income, and the like —and replace it with a cash payment of $3,600 a year to a family of four with no other income. The details are not yet clear, but increases in family income from outside would be supplemented by the federal government until a total income of $7,200 was reached. This proposal appears superior to the Nixon Family Assistance Plan, but a number of important details have yet to be decided. Will there be work requirements? Will the full $3,600 always be provided, even if other government support is provided (for example, old age pensions and social security)? Are there cost-of-living escalation clauses?

Even if President Ford's proposal contains no work requirements, Congress is likely to insert them. Any work requirement would conflict with some basic facts. (1) An OEO study of experimental income guarantees reveals that work requirements are unnecessary. Those on income guarantees do not withdraw from the work force; and in fact, without the threat of economic disaster over their heads, workers are able to seek better-paying and less temporary jobs—thereby reducing their need for welfare.[22] (2) The largest categories of welfare recipients—the old, the blind, children, and single parent families—do not need jobs or job training; they need money to at least adequately support themselves and their families. (Is $3,600 enough?)

It seems likely, then, that future proposals for a guaranteed annual income will create more problems than they solve. The amounts proposed are inadequate, and work requirements would force many people into the unskilled labor market. Poverty would not be eradicated, and it is unlikely that income inequality would be reduced. It is likely that such plans would *increase* inequality in America, while giving the appearance of seriously addressing the problem of poverty.

THE CULTURE OF WELFARE

The welfare system is supported by various beliefs that justify current structural arrangements and reflect dominant values. The American values of achievement, activism, and materialism provide criteria that stress the desirability of competitive efforts in achieving material resources. The values of individualism, freedom, and equality emphasize that individuals should be free to achieve success and thereby make progress for both themselves and society. The value of morality underscores the extent to which Americans assess the worth of individuals according to whether their activities take advantage of the relatively unrestrained opportunities to achieve material success.

Evaluative beliefs represent the concrete application of these abstract criteria to particular social settings. As such, evaluative beliefs indicate what should be and what should occur in particular social contexts. The values of activism, achievement, materialism, progress, freedom, individualism, egalitarianism, and morality provide the criteria for a belief system that we have called the Work Ethic. This ethic, to a very great extent, shapes and guides Americans' conceptions of how wealth and income *should* be distributed.

The Work Ethic

Most Americans fervently believe that efforts to achieve material success should occur within the legitimate occupational structure.[23] Further, a person's income should come from efforts in this sphere; and the amount of income should be roughly proportional to one's skill and ability to take advantage of the opportunities in the American economy. Additionally, all able-bodied individuals—particularly all able-bodied men—

should work. Not only should a man's income come from his work, but his moral worth is related to how hard working he is.[24]

When asked general questions about the Work Ethic, virtually all Americans agree with the tenets just stated. There are some differences among income groups, but there is substantial agreement that each individual's income should come from work and that every able-bodied male should work. One study of the poor—who, in the eyes of many Americans, do not want to work—revealed quite clearly that even the sons of long-term welfare mothers voiced strong desires to work and believed that they would work even if they did not have to. Among poor fathers, the results were the same.[25] Surveys of more affluent populations, whose work has brought some degree of material success, reveal a similar belief in the desirability of work.[26]

The pervasiveness of the Work Ethic helps account for evaluative beliefs about those who do not work. American values of activity, achievement, materialism, progress, freedom, egalitarianism, and individualism provide a moral yardstick with which to assess those who do not work for their incomes. But the potential severity of this assessment of the nonworking is mitigated by the value of humanitarianism, which dictates a more charitable assessment of those who are economically helpless. Humanitarian values and the values that underlie the Work Ethic have become codified into a Welfare Ethic in American society.[27]

The Welfare Ethic
Americans believe in many unfavorable stereotypes about the recipients of welfare payments. These negative attitudes reflect beliefs about what *should* be done with those who do not, or cannot, follow the Work Ethic. The Welfare Ethic emphasizes that no one should take a handout unless absolutely necessary. Income should come from work rather than from charity or the state, but there are circumstances when income assistance is necessary. Welfare should only go to the deserving, who are too young to work, are unable to work for physical reasons, or are temporarily out of work. To accept welfare under any other conditions is to violate the Work Ethic; and those who do so are to be evaluated as morally contemptible.

There appears to be more variability by income groupings in beliefs about the Welfare Ethic than about the Work Ethic. A number of studies reveal that virtually all Americans would prefer to work for their incomes, but among lower-income groups, who are the primary recipients of direct state aid, the acceptance of welfare is not considered as contemptible as it is among middle-income groupings.[28] This acceptance of welfare can be accounted for, at least in part by the perception of the poor that work is unavailable to them. Thus, the acceptance of welfare under these conditions does not violate the tenets of the Work Ethic and meets the deserving-poor tenet of the Welfare Ethic.[29] On the other hand, middle- and upper-income groups believe that work is available to the poor and that those poor who receive welfare do so in violation of both the Welfare and the Work Ethics.[30]

Thus, people's empirical beliefs about "what is" (in this case, availability of work) are shaped by, and in turn, shape evaluative beliefs surrounding welfare. The adherence of the middle- and upper-income groups to the Work and Welfare Ethics forces them to believe that any job—no matter how low paying, demeaning, and temporary—is preferable to welfare. This is a safe belief, because it is unlikely that any of them will ever have to perform such work; but this belief dictates a perception by the affluent that work is available (because low-paying, exhausting, and degrading temporary work is almost always available). Many of the poor, on the other hand, do not always define such jobs as real work, because they offer insufficient income, little future, no security, and are psychologically degrading. Thus, the poor see the receipt of welfare as less undesirable than such jobs when real work is not available.[31]

The power of the Work and Welfare Ethics to force millions of the poor to work is remarkable. Equally remarkable is the capacity of middle-income Americans, whose work is financially rewarding, to condemn welfare recipients as lazy, shiftless, immoral, and dishonest.[32] These varying perceptions of the poor and affluent about reality point to the complexity of the interaction between empirical and evaluative beliefs. For the poor, experience as codified into empirical beliefs shapes their less severe application of evaluative beliefs to themselves. For the affluent, the evaluative beliefs, as sustained by an entirely different work experience, dictates a harsh and negative set of empirical beliefs about the poor. To understand these complex interactions, it is necessary to understand more fully the variations in empirical beliefs held by Americans.

Empirical beliefs represent conceptions about what is and what exists in particular social settings. Such beliefs are, to some extent, tied to people's actual experiences in the world and so beliefs vary somewhat with different life styles. And yet, as has been emphasized, people's experiences are interpreted through the prism of the values and evaluative beliefs they hold. Thus, while we can hypothesize variability among empirical beliefs, it is unlikely that members of different income groups will hold entirely contradictory conceptions of what is, because they maintain similar values and conceptions of what should be. Rather, it would be expected that the more a belief is directly connected to the unique experiences of different income groups, the more divergence in the empirical beliefs of these groups. And conversely, the less directly connected to the unique experiences of different income groups, the more likely are these income groups to hold similar empirical beliefs. As banal as these hypotheses initially appear, they are useful in accounting for variations in Americans' empirical beliefs.

America: the Land of Opportunity . . . for Some. Most people believe that America is a land of vast opportunities. Americans perceive that work is available to those who want it and that education is free for those who are motivated to achieve in school. Even among the poor, who experience inequalities of opportunity, the belief persists that a degree of equal opportunity exists. One study of affluent, middle- and low-income groups in Muskegon, Michigan undertaken in 1966–67 reports that all groups of whites affirm a general belief in the individual's chances to get ahead through hard work.[33] Both middle- and lower-income blacks were considerably more skeptical, and yet a clear majority of both black income groups affirm this belief. But when the questions in this study about opportunity were phrased more concretely, with respect to equal opportunities for job-related income and education, considerably less affirmation of the belief in equal opportunity was evident. This belief has remained strong for at least three decades. A 1945 study of American opinion reported that, while lower-income groups were less optimistic than upper groups, a large majority of all income levels believed that their children's opportunities to rise in the world were as good or better than those of others.[34]

However, Americans also believe that while there is considerable opportunity, some have more opportunity than others to rise. Surveys of public beliefs consistently reveal the recognition that there are barriers to mobility—lack of jobs, discrimination, low pay—for the poor and that the affluent typically have more opportunity than the poor. In the 1945 survey, large minorities of lower income groups perceived that "more opportunities" exist for the rich.[35] In a similar survey conducted in 1969, large minorities of respondents saw low wages, lack of educational equality, and discrimination as factors that inhibit people's chances to be successful.[36]

Thus, members of affluent income groups typically perceive America as the land of equal opportunity, with some qualifications about specific sources of inequality. Members of lower-income groups are more likely to perceive these sources of inequality, but on the whole they still believe that America is a land with vast opportunities. Only black Americans, who are probably in the best position to know, perceive the barriers restricting opportunities. The fact that Americans believe opportunities exist places the burden for failure to achieve on the individual. Although there is a recognition of structural barriers—such as discrimination, low wages, and unequal educational opportunities—the dominant belief asserts that there are opportunities for individuals to seize, if people want to take *advantage* of them. This belief supports the privilege of the affluent who derive the benefits of the current system of income distribution. But equally supportive of the status quo is the slightly diminished belief among the less affluent about equality of opportunity. To have large numbers of those who derive the least from the system believe in equal opportunity is to have them individualize their failure to achieve. This keeps them from attributing their plight to the institutional forces that maintain inequality in the distribution of income. Such implicit individualization of failure to achieve is consistent with the belief in America that individuals are the masters of their own fate.

The Individual in the Land of Opportunity. Most affluent Americans believe that individuals have considerable control over their destinies. Such a belief reflects the strong value of individualism in American culture, but it also mirrors the successful experiences of the affluent in the occupational sphere. In contrast, less affluent Americans recognize the limits on how much an individual can do through sheer desire and hard work.

In a 1945 national public opinion poll, respondents were asked if individual traits such as ability or uncontrollable forces such as luck, pull, or better opportunities were responsible for success and wealth.[37] The most frequent answer was ability, but clear differences among income groups were evident. A large majority of lower-income groups emphasized luck, pull, and better opportunities more than ability. A more recent national survey, conducted in 1969, found that a large majority of Americans emphasize individualistic factors in explaining failure. In comparison to the 1945 poll, differences between income groups were less pronounced.[38]

In the Muskegon, Michigan study, however, individualistic explanations that focused on favorable traits and abilities among the wealthy were pronounced only among the affluent. Poor whites and all blacks remained unconvinced that the wealthy had achieved their affluence through exceptional ability and hard work. Conversely, the affluent saw the plight of the poor as the result of personal failings, whereas the poor perceived that institutional forces prevented their success. But even among the poor, one-third of the white sample saw the material success of the wealthy in terms of positive individual traits and perceived other poor in terms of negative individual characteristics.[39] This finding was confirmed by a Gallup survey of national opinion in 1967, in which respondents were asked: "In your opinion, which is more to blame if a person is poor—lack of effort on his own part or circumstances beyond his control?" Forty-two percent of the entire sample and 30 percent of the poor themselves chose "lack of effort" by the individual as the explanation for economic inequality.

The divergent findings of the few studies of Americans' beliefs about the individual can partially be explained by differences in the samples of respondents and the questions asked of them. But it also seems likely that Americans of different income levels are not equally prone to individualize failure to succeed in the land of opportunity. The less affluent realize that they are not less affluent only because of their personal failings. Nevertheless, one-third to one-half (depending upon which data are used) of the poor see success and failure in terms of personal and individual attributes. This situation helps maintain inequality and preserves the privilege of the affluent by legitimating the current system of income distribution while making a large minority of the poor attribute their plight to the individual and not the system.

The Impoverished: Some Cherished Stereotypes. The belief that individuals can determine their fate in the land of opportunity is codified into a series of beliefs about what makes people poor. The results of several studies indicate that four personal failings are most likely to be attributed to the poor:[40] (1) laziness and lack of motivation, (2) lack of ability, (3) inability to manage money, and (4) drunkenness and loose morals. Again, the lower-income groups are less likely to hold this concept of the poor, but large minorities of the poor support these beliefs. And in at least one community study, poor blacks were more severe in their indictments of the poor than were affluent whites.[41]

Affluent Americans appear to use the criteria of America's dominant values, as codified into evaluative beliefs, to construct a set of empirical beliefs that stereotype the poor as lazy, unmotivated, immoral, and inept. Some poor appear to do the same thing, but a majority recognize the objective barriers to achievement and success in American society. And yet, public opinion surveys reveal that a majority of Americans probably believe at least part of this stereotype—a fact that has profound political implications for how the poor are treated in various institutional spheres.[42]

The Welfare Recipient. Unfavorable beliefs concerning the poor are compounded by a related set of beliefs about welfare recipients. Various national and community studies indicate that a majority, or close to it, of Americans believe that: (1) too many people on welfare are dishonestly representing their need; (2) most could work if they really wanted to; (3) many mothers on welfare have babies to increase their welfare payments. All of these beliefs are objectively incorrect.[43] Less than one-half of those who are eligible for welfare utilize its benefits, and dishonesty is a minor problem; most welfare recipients are disabled, aged, or mothers with preschool children; and welfare payments are too low to make having babies profitable.

Why are these empirical beliefs held by Americans? As long as Americans value achievement, activity, success, progress, freedom, egalitarianism, individualism, and a moral orientation to the world, humanitarian values will always be conditional. The Work and Welfare Ethics set the conditions in the income distribution sphere on just how welfare should be implemented. These ethics embody an attitude of suspicion in the determination of the worthiness of individuals to receive income from other than work activities. This suspicion generates extensive monitoring of the activities of welfare recipients. Monitoring inevitably exposes occasional abuses of welfare "privileges," and the publicity given such abuses confirms the public's "worst suspicions." One result is even more extensive monitoring of "welfare cheaters." This cyclical process facilitates codification of empirical beliefs about welfare recipients that bear little relation to the actual situation of the poor. But as we have seen, these widespread public beliefs have far-reaching consequences for limiting welfare programs and for maintaining the overall pattern of inequality in America.

The Wealthy. Much of the negative opinion and inaccurate beliefs about the poor is related to general ignorance of the wealthy. For the masses of affluent, the poor appear more interesting than the rich, primarily because the poor are economically and politically more vulnerable to scrutiny. If the abuses of wealthfare for the rich—their lack of productive activity and achievement, and their status as recipients of institutional benefits no less real than those received by welfare clients— were more widely known, then perhaps the poor would not be the subject of so many unfavorable beliefs or stereotypes.

The 1945 survey revealed that a large minority perceived the wealthy to have more ability than the poor. But significant percentages of the sample, reaching a large majority in lower-income groups, emphasized that other factors, such as luck, pull, or better opportunities, accounted for the privilege of the affluent.[44] Similar results were obtained in the Muskegon, Michigan study.[45]

Although the lack of data on attitudes about the wealthy make safe generalizations difficult, it seems clear that the general public, especially the lower-income groups, have doubts about how hard the wealthy work to achieve their privilege. But remarkably, none of the intense negative stereotyping, so typical of beliefs about the poor and the welfare recipient, is evident for the wealthy. The wealthy are not seen as violating the Work Ethic, and they are not characterized as lazy, inept, immoral, and excessively dishonest. This absence of negative attitudes about the wealthy enables them to control 40 to 50 percent of the income in the United States and to hoard their privilege without apparently generating much public outrage. The poor, with only 5 percent of the total wealth, are vilified by a series of unfavorable empirical beliefs. The fact that the few relevant surveys have examined public attitudes toward the poor and welfare recipients, rather than public attitudes toward the wealthy, reflects the obsession of the public and of social scientists with what people think about the lower income groups. American values, as codified into a Work Ethic, selectively influence empirical beliefs in such a way as to force scrutiny and distrust of the poor, while the affluent escape serious indictment. This skewed set of empirical beliefs helps legitimate and maintain the institutional arrangements promoting the grossly unequal distribution of income in America.

The Inevitability of Poverty and Inequality. Americans accept inequality and poverty as inevitable. Further, the public appears to have a fairly accurate conception of how many impoverished individuals live in the United States. In the 1969 national survey, the governmental poverty line of $3,500 for a family of four was not considered too high, because four-fifths of the respondents saw such an income as indeed leading to impoverishment.[46] In fact, an income of $4,500 for a four person family in 1969 was still seen by a majority as qualifying a family for the poverty category. Additionally, almost one-half of the respondents guessed that 10 to 20 percent of the population was poor—a guess that corresponded with official government estimates at the time.

Americans thus recognize accurately what income levels propel people into poverty and just how many people are forced to live at or below those levels. Although a large majority agree that the government *should* do something about poverty, only a small minority would be willing to pay higher taxes to finance the effort.[47] Thus, Americans seem willing to accept widespread poverty.

Why is this true? The answer would seem to lie in empirical beliefs about the poor as these beliefs are filtered through dominant values and evaluative beliefs. If one believes that action is to be assessed in terms of values such as activism, achievement, individualism, freedom, and others alluded to earlier, that people should therefore derive income from work and stay off welfare, and that America is a land of opportunity in which individuals are masters of their own fates and failure to seize opportunities is the result of character flaws, then poverty is inevitable because "you can't legislate people's morals and make them work when they don't want to." Further, "it's their own fault" if they are poor, and we "should not subsidize failure and ineptitude with government handouts."

Thus, the values and evaluative beliefs that appear to foster inaccurate beliefs—about opportunities in America, about the capacity of individuals to shape their destinies, and about the flaws of the poor—also enable Americans to see inequality, and particularly poverty, as perhaps regrettable but nonetheless inevitable. As long as inequality and impoverishment are believed to be conditions about which little can be done, then there will be little public pressure to change institutional arrangements that sustain the plight of the poor.

In reviewing the system of ideas surrounding welfare and income distribution in America, we have seen that dominant values, evaluative beliefs, and empirical beliefs interact with each other and society in extremely complex ways. Dominant values provide the criteria for conceiving what *should* exist, while evaluative beliefs distort conceptions, especially among the upper- and middle-income groups, about what *is*. Actual social structural conditions and experiences with these conditions appear to have the most influence on the empirical beliefs, particularly among the poor. And yet, even among a large proportion of low income groups, dominant values and evaluative beliefs distort the perceptions of the poor about their own plight and that of their fellow impoverished.

The limited data must be interpreted cautiously. However, it seems clear that ideas about inequality legitimate the welfare system and its consequences for the plight of the impoverished. This system of ideas convinces the affluent that they deserve what they have and stigmatizes the poor for not being more successful. The tragedy is that this system of ideas also regulates the perceptions of large numbers of the poor, keeping them psychologically stigmatized as failures in the land of opportunity.

In Figure 1, we have summarized the complex relationships among ideas, the welfare system, and inequality. The dominant values have become translated into Work and Welfare Ethics that shape, and are reinforced by, a series of empirical beliefs that individualize the failure of the poor and stigmatize them. These values and beliefs are used to legitimate, and are in turn supported by, the current "grants and aids" welfare system. Such beliefs are also likely to restrict any guaranteed income or negative tax proposal enacted by Congress. Whether through the current system or some future income guarantee, welfare will promote persistent poverty.

The double arrows emphasize that structural arrangements often make ideas self-fulfilling, because the system is set up to deal with the poor as if they were lazy and unwilling to work. But when the poor are treated this way, they naturally resist efforts to force them into ungratifying

Figure 1: The Welfare System

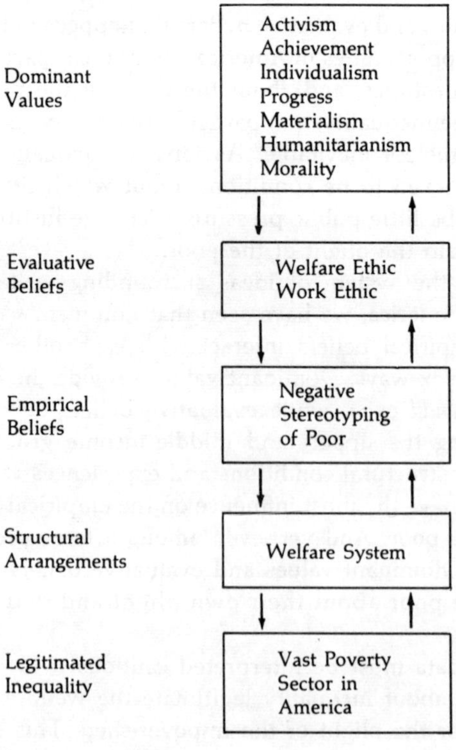

Dominant Values	Activism Achievement Individualism Progress Materialism Humanitarianism Morality
Evaluative Beliefs	Welfare Ethic Work Ethic
Empirical Beliefs	Negative Stereotyping of Poor
Structural Arrangements	Welfare System
Legitimated Inequality	Vast Poverty Sector in America

work. Further, appeals to values and beliefs are easily made by political figures. Politicians have little to fear from the poor; they must court the votes of the affluent masses, and they accept campaign money from the wealthy. If the concern of the general public is focused on "welfare cheaters," attention is diverted away from the affluent and rich recipients of wealthfare—thereby ideologically mobilizing the majority against the poor.

NOTES

1. Only about $17 billion in state, county, and federal money is spent for welfare each year. Contrasted with the $60 to $70 billion spent on the wealthfare dole of the federal government alone—to say nothing of state government's dole—this is not as large a sum as it might initially appear.

2. For a historical treatment of the American case, see Francis Fox Piven and Richard A. Cloward, *Regulating the Poor: The Functions of Public Welfare* (New York: Random House, 1971).

3. Piven and Cloward, *Regulating the Poor*; Ben B. Seligman, *Permanent Poverty: An American Syndrome* (Chicago: Quadrangle Books, 1970); Robert H. Bremer, *From the Depths: The Discovery of Poverty in the United States* (New York: New York University Press, 1956).

4. Sophonisba P. Breckinridge, ed., *Public Welfare Administration in the United States: Select Documents* (Chicago: University of Chicago Press, 1927), pp. 226–227.

5. The following discussion draws heavily from Piven and Cloward's excellent summary (*Regulating the Poor*, pp. 45–122) of changes and cycles of relief given during the Great Depression. For other helpful works, see: Josephine Chapin Brown, *Public Relief 1924–1939* (New York: Henry Holt and Co., 1940); Basil Rauch, *The History of the New Deal 1933–1938* (New York: Creative Age Press, 1944); Emma A. Winslow, *Trends in Different Types of Public and Private Relief in Urban Areas, 1929–1935* (Washington, D.C.: Government Printing Office, 1937); Arthur M. Schlesinger, Jr., *The Age of Roosevelt*, vol. 2 and vol. 3 (Boston: Houghton-Mifflin, 1958 and 1960, respectively).

6. Brown, *Public Relief*, p. 99.

7. Piven and Cloward, *Regulating the Poor*, p. 94.

8. *Ibid.*, p. 117.

9. *Ibid.*, p. 132.

10. For a summary of statistics on poor and welfare recipients, see Jonathan H. Turner, *American Society: Problems of Structure* (New York: Harper and Row, 1972), p. 79. For specific community studies on New York and Detroit, respectively, see: Mignon Sauber and Elaine Rubinstein, *Experiences of Unwed Mothers as Parents* (New York: Community Council of Greater New York, 1965); and Greenlight Associates, *Study of Services to Deal with Poverty in Detroit* (New York: Greenlight Associates, 1965).

11. For summaries of several studies documenting these kinds of abuses, see Piven and Cloward, *Regulating the Poor*, pp. 152–156.

12. *Ibid.*, p. 158.

13. These statements should not imply that more socialistic economies are not also subject to similar cycles. However, these cycles are typically less severe and not the result of purely technical factors of supply and demand in the market. Further, because government control of the economy is more extensive, recessions can be more easily controlled and their impact on the population more readily mitigated.

14. Jonathan H. Turner, *American Society: Problems of Structure*, rev. ed (New York: Harper and Row, 1976).

15. Dorothy Projector and Gertrude Weiss, *Survey of Financial Characteristics of Consumers*, (Washington, D.C.: Federal Reserve Technical Papers, August 1966), pp. 126–138.

16. Howard P. Tuckman, *The Economics of the Rich* (New York: Random House, 1973), p. 166. This volume is probably the most readable and comprehensive analysis by an economist of the inequalities built into the economic, legal, and educational sectors of

the society. We will have occasion to draw from this insightful analysis at several points in this chapter and the next.

17. *Ibid.,* p. 162.

18. *Federal Reserve Bulletin,* May 1973.

19. Tuckman, *Economics of the Rich,* p. 149.

20. Paul Jacobs, "Keeping the Poor Poor," in *Crisis in American Institutions,* ed. Jerome H. Skolnick and Elliott Currie (Boston: Little Brown, 1970), pp. 42–52.

21. Turner, *American Society.*

22. Office of Economic Opportunity, *Further Preliminary Results of the New Jersey Work Incentive Experiment* (Washington, D.C.: Government Printing Office, 1971).

23. The Work Ethic has been a frequent topic of study. See, for example: Joe R. Feagin, "Poverty: We still Believe that God Helps Those Who Help Themselves," *Psychology Today,* 6 (November 1972): 101 ff.; Leonard Goodwin, *Do the Poor Want to Work?: A Social-Psychological Study of Work Orientations* (Washington, D.C.: The Brookings Institution, 1972); Richard Centers, "Attitude and Belief in Relation to Occupational Stratification," *Journal of Social Psychology,* 27 (May 1948): 159–185; and Joan Huber and William H. Form, *Income and Ideology: An Analysis of the American Political Formula* (New York: Free Press, 1973).

24. With respect to women in the work force, these values are applied selectively. For the poor family with a woman as the head, the woman should work at menial jobs such as cleaning floors. For the middle-class widowed or divorced woman, work is not considered as essential.

25. Goodwin, *Do the Poor Want to Work?;* David J. Kallen and Dorothy Miller, "Public Attitudes toward Welfare," *Social Work,* 16 (July 1971): 83–90.

26. Feagin, "Poverty: We Still Believe"; Huber and Form, *Income and Ideology.*

27. Feagin, "Poverty: We Still Believe"; Goodwin, *Do the Poor Want to Work?*

28. Huber and Form, *Income and Ideology;* Goodwin, *Do the Poor Want to Work?*

29. Goodwin, *Do the Poor Want to Work?*

30. Feagin, "Poverty: We Still Believe"; Feagin, Joe R., "America's Welfare Stereotypes," *Social Science Quarterly,* 52 (March 1972): 921–933.

31. Goodwin, *Do the Poor Want to Work?*

32. Huber and Form, *Income and Ideology.*

33. Huber and Form, *Income and Ideology,* pp. 90–91.

34. Centers, "Attitude and Belief."

35. *Ibid.*

36. Feagin, "America's Welfare Stereotypes."

37. Centers, "Attitude and Belief."

38. Feagin, "Poverty: We Still Believe."

39. Huber and Form, *Income and Ideology.*

40. Centers, "Attitude and Belief"; Feagin, "Poverty: We Still Believe"; and Huber and Form, *Income and Ideology.*

41. Kallen and Miller, "Public Attitudes."

42. Feagin, "America's Welfare Stereotypes"; Huber and Form, *Income and Ideology.*

43. See, for documentation: Feagin, "Poverty: We Still Believe"; and Turner, *American Society.*

44. Centers, "Attitude and Belief."

45. Huber and Form, *Income and Ideology.*

46. Feagin, "Poverty: We Still Believe."

47. *Ibid.*

8
A MODEL
OF INEQUALITY

THE SYSTEM OF PRIVILEGE AND POVERTY
IN AMERICA

It is now possible to visualize the overall impact of cultural and structural forces on patterns of inequality in America. We have argued that inequality is perpetuated by the dual welfare and wealthfare establishments. In Table 1, we have summarized the profile of these two systems. As can be seen by reading down the welfare and wealthfare columns, wealthfare recipients receive more money. They receive it via indirect routes so that they are not stigmatized for being on the "government dole." The vast majority of the population receive wealthfare; the bottom income fifth receives welfare. Those who receive wealthfare are more likely to be the subjects of favorable stereotypes, while the reverse is true for welfare recipients. There are many ways to be eligible for wealthfare, few for welfare. And monitoring of wealthfare recipients is not as severe as it is for welfare recipients.

These differences in the operation of the wealthfare and welfare systems are reflections of differences in the political power of different segments of the economy. The vast majority of Americans do enjoy some degree of affluence, and they support the system that bestows *some* privilege on them. The very wealthy, however, derive *vast* privilege from this same system, a fact that is only vaguely perceived by the affluent majority and about which they are prepared to do very little. For the poor, who are a minority and who have little power, only the welfare system is available. The poor and the affluent majority have a long-term interest

Table 1 The Welfare and Wealthfare Systems

	Wealthfare	Welfare
(1) Source of Subsidy	Market purchases by government Government price policies Government export-import policies Government tax expenditures	Federal "grants and aids," supplemented by state and country subsidies
(2) Amount of Subsidy	Unknown for government economic policies, but probably at least 50 billion 60–70 billion in tax expenditures	15–20 billion by federal, state, and local governments
(3) Recipients of Subsidy	Middle and upper income fifths; the more you make, the more you get	Bottom income fifth; the less you make, the more you get
(4) Stereotypes Associated with recipients	Decent, hard-working people and/or clever entrepreneurs who know how to work the system	Lazy, immoral people who do not know how to manage their finances and who do not want to work
(5) Eligibility Requirements for Subsidy	Work for a large corporation which does a lot of business with government; belong to a large union or professional association; own large shares of stock in large corporations doing business with government; and have a good tax lawyer fill out complicated forms provided by government	Be close to starving; have kids; have a physical deformity; lose your job; or be old
(6) Monitoring of Recipients	Proclamations by President's Council of Economic Advisers on the "state of the economy"; spot checking by IRS	Frequent checking by "eligibility" worker who visits your home

in redistributing the privilege of the wealthy, but they are much more likely to see each other as enemies than to perceive the rich as their enemies. And so they consolidate the power and privilege of the wealthy.

The cultural and structural forces that divide the poor and affluent while preserving the privilege of the rich are highly complex. Economic and political arrangements as they have created the welfare and wealthfare establishments have complex, reciprocal relationships not only with each other, but also with systems of beliefs and values. It is this latter set of relationships with cultural values and beliefs that diverts the attention of most Americans away from their true interests and makes the dual systems of wealthfare and welfare appear legitimate and proper. In Figure 1, we summarize the key relationships among the social and cultural forces that perpetuate the coexistence of privilege and poverty in America.

Figure 1 is a composite model of relationships among cultural and structural forces discussed in previous chapters. As such, it can be viewed as a summary of our arguments about how and why vast inequality

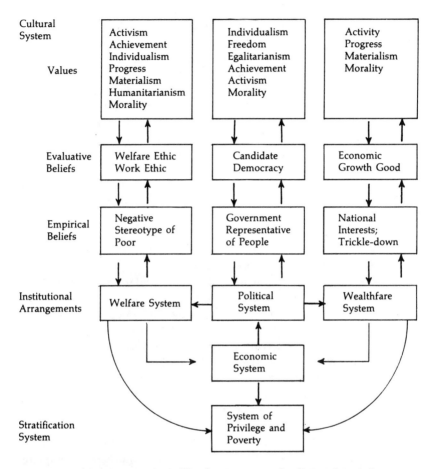

Figure 1 A Model of Inequality in America

Cultural System			
Values	Activism Achievement Individualism Progress Materialism Humanitarianism Morality	Individualism Freedom Egalitarianism Achievement Activism Morality	Activity Progress Materialism Morality
Evaluative Beliefs	Welfare Ethic Work Ethic	Candidate Democracy	Economic Growth Good
Empirical Beliefs	Negative Stereotype of Poor	Government Representative of People	National Interests; Trickle-down
Institutional Arrangements	Welfare System	Political System	Wealthfare System
		Economic System	
Stratification System		System of Privilege and Poverty	

persists in American society. The key structural relationship is between the economy and polity, and it is in this relationship that the affluent and wealthy segments of the economy are able to exert political power. This exercise of power is legitimated by empirical beliefs, evaluative beliefs, and certain dominant values, as outlined in Figure 1. The values of freedom, individualism, egalitarianism, achievement, activism, and morality have become codified into beliefs in the appropriateness of a candidate as opposed to party system—the candidate system is seen as representative of the will of the people. Such cultural orientations, we have argued, make the political process highly vulnerable to disproportionate influence by the wealthy. As the reciprocal arrows in Figure 1 emphasize, the power elite (to overstate the case for emphasis) actively promotes the perpetuation of the very beliefs and values which support its power.

The respective political influences of the poor, the affluent, and the rich have resulted in the creation of the welfare and wealthfare systems which, like all enduring social structures, are legitimated by empirical beliefs, evaluative beliefs, and some dominant values. With respect to the welfare system, dominant values of activism, achievement, individualism, progress, materialism, humanitarianism, and morality have become codified into Work and Welfare Ethics, which have led to a series of negative empirical beliefs about the poor. In turn, the welfare system fulfills its own prophecy by instituting programs that provide low levels of subsidy, abuse the poor, and force or induce them into the unskilled labor market. And thus, when the poor "act poor," or appear "demoralized" or "lazy" in their no-win situation, the affluent majority can actively support those values and beliefs which legitimate the present welfare system.

In regard to the wealthfare system, values of activism, progress, materialism, and morality have become translated into an evaluative belief in economic growth which, in turn, has been codified into empirical beliefs about national interest and trickle down. Because these beliefs promote privilege, the wealthy actively support their perpetuation, as is indicated by the double arrows in Figure 1.

As the arrows between the wealthfare and welfare systems and the political and economic systems indicate, the wealthfare and welfare systems promote inequality by subsidizing the affluent and wealthy sectors of the economy and forcing the poor to participate in the most competitive, menial, low paying, and economically insecure occupations. But as the arrows from the welfare and wealthfare systems to the stratification system emphasize, privilege and poverty are directly affected by these two systems, without reference to economic processes. For example, the low welfare payments maintain poverty, while tax expenditures directly subsidize privilege.

In reviewing the complex relationships among cultural and social structures, it is evident that the model presented in Figure 1 is incomplete. One problem with the model is that casual priority is specified only for the influence of economic forces on political processes and for the creation of the dual welfare and wealthfare systems. No causal priorities are established for relationships between cultural and social variables, nor is a priority specified for the direct and indirect (through the economy) impact of welfare and wealthfare establishments on the system of privilege and poverty. Essentially, all that we have said is: Power is determined by a group's economic position; with power, different economic groups can preserve their privilege and force those without power to live in poverty; these processes can be legitimated by values and beliefs that those with power can actively seek to disseminate.

The indebtedness of this argument to Marx, Lenski, and others is obvious. What is missing is a *theory* of how one set of variables causes variations in others. The model in Figure 1 specifies that relationships exist, but it does not adequately indicate the respective strengths of relationships. The model helps in visualizing the variables that must be incorporated into a theory, and so it is a good place to begin constructing theory. But it is not theory, except in the most crude and evocative sense. For students of inequality, then, a model such as Figure 1 can, when combined with other models for other societies, serve as a basis for constructing a more comprehensive theory of inequality. The analysis presented in the preceding chapters is, thus, only a first step in what will be a long process of theoretical reflection.

REDUCING INEQUALITY IN AMERICA: A CONCLUDING COMMENTARY

Throughout this book, two seemingly contradictory messages have been communicated: (1) inequality is inevitable, and more implicitly, (2) inequality is bad. Our scholarly analysis and understanding of systems of inequality in present and past societies leads us to the conclusion that inequality is inevitable. And our moral judgements about the consequences of inequality for various segments of a society's population forces us to consider it as one of the less desirable features of human social organization. To assess as morally bad what is inevitable is, of course, to invite considerable psychological dissonance; and thus, many thinkers, such as Marx, have sought to resolve this dissonance by postulating future utopias in which economic resources would be equally distributed.

Although the authors of such postulations often document their hopes, as Marx did, with extensive scholarship, they nonetheless fly in the face of the hard facts: All known societies that have some economic surplus reveal economic inequality. Very simple hunting and gathering societies have little inequality, primarily because they do not have much surplus. And in some societies, such as Masai tribes in Africa, people are able to move in and out of privileged positions during their life cycles. But in all large-scale, modern, and industrial societies, inequality is a fact of social life. The future is always subject to hopeful speculation, but inequality is likely to be with us for many generations. It is in light of this situation that what probably has been considered a radical analysis of inequality turns out to be more pessimistic than radical. Such a conclusion is, in many ways, justified, for the analysis has focused on the powerful sociocultural forces perpetuating a system of privilege and poverty in America.

Our own internalizations of the values of progress, humanitarianism, and morality lead us to offer some indication of how *reductions* in inequality are possible. Inequality cannot be eliminated, but the degree of inequality can be reduced. Reduction in inequality, however, will require some radical changes in the structure and culture of American society.

The key to initiating change in the system of inequality is the political organization not just of the poor but also of the many affluent, who would fare much better with redistribution of resources in America. The major organizational obstacle is the perception of the affluent that the poor are their enemies. If this obstacle is to be overcome, massive alterations must be made in the empirical beliefs, and perhaps, in the evaluative beliefs and values held by the affluent. Such changes are not easily accomplished, but they are possible when it is demonstrated that self-interest dictates change. America has witnessed dramatic changes in beliefs about war, voting age, abortion, women, deviance, and other issues, and it is possible to contemplate change in beliefs about the poor and about *wealth*fare. Persistent exposure of wealthfare abuses and clear documentation that the elimination of wealthfare would not destroy the American way of life might enable the majority—say the bottom three income fifths—to accept socially responsible activities of lobbying organizations. It would be difficult, of course, to convince people that the medical, interest, and other deductions that they now enjoy are not in their best interests and that taxes could be reduced and greater equality and equity in America would prevail if these and other wealth-fare tax expenditures were eliminated. To counteract the power of well-organized organizations that benefit from the wealthfare system, money and organization to wage media campaigns and finance lobbying organizations in the capital would be required.

The political system must be used rather than changed. Organization and money—especially organization of the majority—will be the most effective weapons in a war against privilege. With these resources it would be possible to influence Americans to become as skeptical about wealthfare as they currently are about welfare. By competing with, rather than being co-opted by, the wealthy and their organizations, the majority could eliminate at least some wealthfare abuses. The money collected in this way could be used to increase welfare benefits, to provide higher wages in existing jobs, and to create public service jobs. These changes would reduce some of the privilege of the wealthy and much of the poverty of the poor. The middle groups would probably be relatively unaffected by these changes as the income and wealth levels began to regress toward the middle income and wealth fifths.

All that can be expected in the future, then, is a lessening of inequality. Capitalism, as many utopians hope and believe, is not about to crumble in the coming decades. Even if more collectivist forms of economic organization increased in the modern world, they too would establish their own systems of privilege and poverty. Pressuring government to initiate changes in the welfare and wealthfare systems is a more useful strategy than waiting for the demise of capitalism.

The changes proposed could reduce inequality and eliminate abject poverty while limiting excessive privilege. To hope for more would be to pursue an illusion. To wait for *the* economic and political collapse that will usher in some new, more equitable utopia would be to accept implicitly a highly abusive system of privilege and poverty in America. To pursue what is possible is ultimately more psychologically rewarding and more humane for those in abject poverty. It is for this reason that our analysis of inequality in America was initiated. Hopefully, it begins to expose the welfare and wealthfare systems for what they are.

INDEX

A

Achievement as a dominant
American value, 69, 70, 140
Activism as a dominant American
value, 69–70, 140
Aid to Families with Dependent
Children (AFDC), 127, 129
American Revolution. *See*
Revolutionary War
Amortization, short-term, 97
Aristotle as ideologist of middle
class, 6
Assets, 25–27
investment, 25, 26, 30
liquid, 25
miscellaneous, 25, 28
Assumption Act, 14
Auto equity, 27–30

B

Baltimore, distribution of wealth in
(1860), 18, 22
Baltimore, Lord, 12
Beard, Charles Austin, 13

Beliefs, 66–67
"national interest," 115–116, 117
systems of, 67–68
"trickle down," 116–117
Bonds, investment in, 43
Burke, Edmund, 65
Byrd family of Virginia, 12

C

Candidate democracies, 76, 86
Capital gains, 98–99
Capitalism
economic cycles associated with,
131–132
economic requirements of, 124
disparities of wealth and, 44–45
laissez-faire, 124
Carter, Robert, 13
Charity, 71, 122. *See also*
Humanitarianism *and*
Relief-giving
Charles I (1600–1649), King of
England, 12
Civilian Conservation Corps, 126